Soup Maker Cookbook:

Discover The Secrets Of Our Ancestors' Winter Flavors With Creamy, Flavorful Recipes For All Palates

Copyright © 2022

Sarah Roslin

TABLE OF CONTENTS

1 INTRODUCTION

Soup is one of the universal forms of the way food is cooked. You would find that there are various forms of soup throughout various cuisines in the world. Soup can come in the form of Wonton Soup from your local Chinese takeout, to the more classical types such as your French Onion Soup. Soup is a familiar food to many of us as we associate with warmth and comfort, and when we do become ill, there is nothing more comfortable than a bowl of hot soup with a slice of bread or crackers to dip into the bowl.

Comfort aside, you would find soup to be a mainstay in many households, and each person would resort to a bowl of soup every once in a while. Soups are easy to prepare and can often come packed with the nutritional requirements that your body needs in a single bowl. They can be thin, flavorful broths or the rich, creamy potages that really stick to your ribs. Not to mention you have a whole inventory of soups to choose from in accordance with what you happen to be in the mood for. Summer? Have some corn chowder. Winter? Have some nice, thick butternut squash soup. Soups are an adaptable form of cuisine that can make the most of your desire and make the most of what is in your pantry at home.

Soup making has become easier what with the advent of the soup maker. You do not have to act like a cordon bleu chef and continuously stir and skim stock for your soup base, as this modern technological marvel does all the work for you. Now, if you simply want to have your soup, all you have to do is use your soup maker and you can have comfort in a bowl anytime you want it.

This cookbook would serve as a guide for you to have the soups that you want at any time with the aid of your soup maker. So we get to the heart of the book first, what is a soup maker?

1.1 What is a Soup Maker?

From the name alone you can already tell that a soup maker is simply a kitchen appliance that allows you to make soup. So what makes it different from a slow cooker or an Insta-Pot? Well, these latter appliances are not devoted to the exclusive use of soups and you would need to constantly watch the ingredients that you add into them to ensure that they end up as soup and not as a sauce among other things. Think of the soup maker as a specialized machine that allows you to make soup. They are designed after all, to help you cook tasty soups without the need to constantly supervise the said appliance. As you would with a bread machine, all you have to do is add the ingredients into the container and the machine will make the soup for you.

You would, of course have to chop ingredients before you add them in. You can hardly add an entire carrot or potato and expect the machine to peel and chop them for you. What you have to do with prep, the machine makes up for with the rest as you do not have to stir all the time. A look at your soup maker will show that it has different settings to accommodate the type and texture of soup that you would wish to do. This statement is not universal however, as you can expect that each soup maker would have different settings for each model.

It is expected that there are some soup makers that can blend food items similar to how you would expect gazpacho and other blended soups. Similarly, you can find soup makers with settings that allow you to blend your soup according to texture: soups therefore can be chunky to smooth or whichever happens to be your personal preference. Aside from texture though, you can expect that there would be variations in temperature, along with controls to determine how long your soup is expected to be cooked. More sophisticated models of soup makers can have your soup ready to serve in twenty minutes, whereas more basic models can take longer- though admittedly still hands-free.

You will need to consider the capacity of your soup maker. Soup makers are not all made equal, as you can tell with the difference in the functionalities. Some soup makers are able to serve a family of four, so you would have to make adjustments to know how much soup you would like to consume, or how much you can actually keep. Soup, nourishing as it is, cannot be the mainstay of your entire meal for all time.

1.2 Advantages of a Soup Maker

Despite the choices that you have to make when you purchase your soup maker, the machine makes up for its expense with the amount of time you save. Once you have prepared the ingredients and added them into the machine, you are able to get a quick and hot meal within half an hour. You can spend the extra time you have to catch up with work, or relax in the comforts of your home while you wait for a comforting bowl of soup.

Another advantage is the ease with which you are able cook soup. Once your ingredients have been prepped, all you have to do is add them into the soup maker and set the time and temperature and you are done. You do not need to have extraordinary kitchen skills to make soup. Specialized models allow the soup maker to remember particular settings which can come useful especially if you are tired. If you are not ready to eat yet, your soup maker would be able to keep your soup warm for you. This ensures that your soup is ready to eat without the potential to overcook it or to let it cook dry. It also helps you save on your gas bill in the end as you do not have to reheat soup anymore, the machine keeps it warm for you. Soup makers come with multiple functions as mentioned throughout this chapter. Some soup makers come with a built-in blender option, so soup recipes that require the use of a blender before the soup is cooked save an extra step and allow you do to these recipes in a single machine. There is no need to pour and transfer soup from one container to another. Aside from soup, your soup maker would be able to cook other dishes, although this functionality is limited to the model of soup maker that you have, so be sure to check your manual. Because your soup maker comes with added functionalities, you are able to save on counter space and clean up would be a breeze with a one-pot meal.

Ultimately, soup makers are well worth the investment as it allows you make soups with fresh ingredients. You do not have to spend for prepackaged soup mixes, canned soups and other processed products that may also be harmful to your health if consumed frequently. Freshly made soup with fresh ingredients can now be easily done with the aid of your soup maker which would bring your grocery bill down and help you save more money.

1.3 The Lowdown on Soup Makers

Soup makers are not complicated to use and are quite simple once you get accustomed to it. Once you do, you can make soups for every day of the year if you choose to do so. You would have to follow the instructions in the recipes that will come in the subsequent chapters however, as there are limits to what the soup maker can actually prep and cook for you. Once your ingredients have been prepared in accordance with the instructions on the recipes, simply add them into the pot.

The next step is dependent on your soup maker, as it can be an LED Display or a series of buttons. You would have to follow the instructions on the recipe as to what settings should you use for a particular recipe. There are several options for soup makers, again, in accordance with each model. However, standard settings for soup makers include these three:

- Chunky – an option used if you prefer, or if the recipe calls for, a blended soup with enough chunks left to give texture to the soup. You may use this in gazpacho for instance.

- Smooth – an option if you prefer soups with a smooth texture, as with cream-based soups and blended root vegetable soups.
- Cool – a more multifunctional option, this setting is suitable not only for cold soups, but also for smoothies, dips and other sauces as the soup maker may accommodate.

Some soup makers may have a memory function as mentioned earlier in this book. They may be pricier models, true, but are well worth the investment if you find yourself tired after a long day at work, and have your recipes memorized by rote. All you have to do at this point is to chuck the ingredients into the soup maker and press the memory settings and relax.

Once you have chosen the kind of soup that you wish to do, all you have to do is adjust the temperature of your soup maker. There are either up and down arrows or a +/- sign to indicate if the temperature has been increased or decreased. These same symbols are also used to adjust the time, and all you would need to do is adjust the time to how long the soup is supposed to cook according to the instructions of the recipe.

The Keep Warm functionality allows your soup maker to keep your soup warm while you attend to other tasks. This saves you on your energy bill to reheat the soup as your soup is kept warm for you. Best of all, you do not need to rush to check on your soup as it will remain warm without the risk of evaporating the liquid.

Some soup makers can burn however, especially if they happen to be older models. If you are fond of soup, an upgrade may be worth the price, especially with the added functionalities as mentioned in the book.

Your Soup Maker is easy to clean, as you can simply allow it to soak with hot, soapy water for about fifteen minutes, before you carefully scrub out the insides with an abrasive sponge – you may want to recheck your manual on more thorough instructions on how to clean your soup maker as it may potentially void your warranty. This method also applies in the event that your soup maker has burned bits at the bottom that simply refuse to come off no matter how much you scrape it.

1.4 Quick and Easy How To's for Soup Makers

You can expect that you would have to do some prep work before you add your ingredients to your soup. You can prepare certain ingredients ahead of time, especially if they keep well, otherwise ingredients that turn brown rapidly, such as potatoes, should be prepped just before you add them into the soup maker. If you are in a rush, you can use frozen prepared vegetables such as peas.

To save on time, you can also use preheated stocks or preheated water just before you add these into the soup maker. This way, your soup is already underway and you would have a more flavorful result. Not to mention, the heated stock would also help you cook tougher vegetables such as potatoes and carrots as it waits for your soup maker to heat up. If you use vegetables that are hard, such as potatoes, carrots, squash, beets, turnips and other root vegetables, you want to cut them into a smaller dice to ensure that they are able to cook faster within the time limit set by the recipe. In a similar vein, be sure that the meat you add into your soup maker has been thoroughly cooked. Soup makers do not heat long enough to ensure that your meat has been well cooked.

Lastly, once you have chopped and added all of your ingredients, be sure to keep the lid shut tightly to help it build up heat. To avoid burned meat stuck at the bottom of the pot of the soup maker, be sure to only add these if the pot has been filled halfway with stock or water. The stickiness occurs from the contact of the meat with the bottom of the heated pot. Add the remainder of the ingredients next. Frozen ingredients must be thawed first before you add them. Do not let them thaw while in the soup maker as this would not only increase the volume of the liquid inside, but also dilute the flavor that you worked hard to build. Additionally, if this is a blended soup, frozen items may damage the blade of the soup maker.

While your soup cooks, do not open the lid. The hot liquid may splash and cause burns. As you clean the soup maker, do not soak the lid or any other part that has an electrical component otherwise you will permanently damage your soup maker.

Due to the nature of the contents of the soup maker, it is imperative that you follow safety precautions for a risk free soup maker.

- Do not fill up your soup maker more than halfway beyond the minimum and maximum indicators on your pot.
- Your soup maker or any of its components, especially electronic components should never be submerged in water. Kindly consult your manual before you clean your soup maker to ensure your warranty does not become void.
- Keep your soup makers away from the edges of the counter and do not leave the wires hanging where children are able to reach them. This should be constant, especially if you have children at home.
- While the soup cooks, do not open the lid as mentioned earlier in this chapter. If you do get burned by the liquid, wash the area underneath cool water and apply first aid for burns.
- Do not use your soup maker to reheat soups that are already pre-made or store-bought. Its settings are ideal for freshly made soup.

1.5 Conclusion

Soup is a highly nutritious dish that allows you take in nutritionally dense food with the use of a spoon. The use of a soup maker makes it an ideal helpmate especially if you are fond of soup as a quick meal, or as part of your unique dietary requirements. There are certain steps on how to navigate the use of a soup maker if you are a first time owner, but one you get the hang of it, you are able to make soups 365 days a year if you choose to do so. If you use your soup maker properly, it becomes a useful kitchen helpmate and a workhorse in the kitchen. Take care of it, and it will help you produce soups without the need for complex preparations. If you feel you are ready to embark on a culinary journey one bowl at a time, take a gander at the next chapter to see how to set up your pantry for soup making success and get started on the recipes of this cookbook.

2 VEGETARIAN SOUPS

2.1 Potato-Chickpea Potage

Serves: 4 Preparation Time: 5 minutes Cooking Time: 28 minutes

Ingredients:

- Chickpeas, 1 can (14 oz.), rinsed and drained
- Onion, 1 small, finely chopped
- Potatoes, medium-sized , 2 pieces, peeled and chopped
- Coriander Seed, ground, 1 **tsp.**
- Cumin, ground -1 **tsp.**
- Turmeric, ground - ½ **tsp.**
- Cayenne Pepper - 1/8 **tsp.**
- Salt
- Black Pepper, freshly ground
- Lemon Juice, freshly squeezed – 2 **tbsp.**s
- Vegetable Broth – 3 cups, hot
- Parsley, fresh – 2 **tbsp.**s

Procedure:

1. Add all of the ingredients into the soup maker, except for the parsley.
2. Shut the lid tightly and choose the chunky setting and set the time for 28 minutes.
3. Once the soup has been fully cooked, carefully unlatch the lid and transfer the soup into individual bowls. Garnish with the parsley.

Nutritional Facts: Cal: 414; Carb: 81.7g; Protein: 14.2g; Fat: 10g; Fiber: 15.7g; Sugars: 17.1g; Cholesterol: 0mg; Sodium: 2808mg

2.2 Chickpea Soup

Serves: 4 Preparation Time: 5 minutes Cooking Time: 28 minutes

Ingredients:

- Olive Oil, 2 **tbsp.**s
- Onion, 1 whole, chopped finely
- Carrot, 1 small piece, peeled and chopped
- Celery, 1 stalk, chopped
- Garlic, 2 cloves, peeled and crushed
- Salt
- Chickpeas, 1 (14.oz) can, rinsed and drained
- Tomatoes, 1 can, diced
- Dried Cumin Seed, ½ **tsp.**, ground
- Cinnamon, ½ **tsp.**, ground
- Paprika, ½ **tsp.**
- Cayenne Pepper, ½ **tsp.**
- Vegetable Broth, 3 cups

Procedure:

1. In a wok pan, heat the olive oil over a medium flame, and sauté the onion, carrot and celery. Add the garlic and sprinkle with salt. Cook until the vegetables are tender and are aromatic, about 5 minutes. This is your mirepoix.
2. Transfer this mirepoix into the Soup Maker and stir in the remainder of the ingredients. Stir to combine. Lock the lid and select the Chunky setting. Set the time for 28 minutes.
3. Once the soup has finished cooking, carefully lift the lid and ladle the soup into bowls. Serve immediately,

Nutritional Facts: Cal: 617; Carb: 70.7g; Protein: 15.7g; Fat: 38.1g; Fiber: 14.7g; Sugars: 18.9g; Cholesterol: 0mg; Sodium: 2795mg

2.3 Traditional Tomato Potage

Serves: 4 Preparation Time: 5 minutes Cooking Time: 30 minutes

Ingredients:

- Tomatoes, 650 grams
- Garlic, 1 clove, peeled and minced
- Onions, 50 grams, peeled and finely chopped
- Vegetable Stock, 2 cups
- Sugar, 1 **tsp.**
- Salt
- Black Pepper, freshly ground
- Basil Leaves, fresh (optional)
- Crème Fraiche to garnish

Procedure:

1. Quarter the tomatoes. Peel the garlic and add these along with the other ingredients except for the basil and the crème fraiche into the Soup Maker.
2. Secure the lid and choose the cream or smooth option and set the time for 30 minutes.
3. Once the soup is fully cooked, carefully transfer the soup into serving bowls and garnish with the basil and a dollop of crème fraiche. Serve immediately with garlic bread if desired.

Nutritional Facts: Cal: 132; Carb: 24.8g; Protein: 2.9g; Fat: 6.9g; Fiber: 3.9g; Sugars: 16.1g; Cholesterol: 5mg; Sodium: 1612mg

2.4 Cannellini and Barley Soup

Serves: 4 Preparation Time: 10 minutes Cooking Time: 38 minutes

Ingredients:

- Olive Oil, 1 **tbsp.**
- Onion, 1 whole, peeled and chopped
- Celery, 1 stalk, finely chopped
- Carrot, 1 small piece, peeled and chopped
- Rosemary, fresh, 1 **tbsp.**, chopped
- Garlic, 2 cloves, peeled and minced
- Tomatoes, 1 cup, chopped
- Vegetable Stock, 3 cups
- Barley, 1 cup, cooked
- Canned Cannellini Beans, 1 ¼ cup, drained and rinsed

- Lemon Juice, 1 **tbsp.**
- Salt
- Black Pepper, freshly ground

Procedure:

1. Heat the oil in a medium saucepan and sauté the onions, carrots and celery for 4 to 5 minutes or until softened and aromatic. Add the garlic and rosemary and continue to sauté for 1 minute. Add the tomatoes and cook for 3 to 4 minutes. Use the back of a wooden spoon to crush the tomatoes.
2. Transfer the mixture into the Soup Maker. Pour in the remainder of the ingredients and stir to combine. Secure the lid and set the soup maker on Chunky for 38 minutes.
3. Once the soup has been fully cooked, carefully unlock the lid and ladle the soup into individual bowls to serve.

Nutritional Facts: Cal: 1707; Carb: 312.1g; Protein: 81.7g; Fat: 26.9g; Fiber: 95.9g; Sugars: 29.9g; Cholesterol: 0mg; Sodium: 2481mg

2.5 Bulgur and Bean Soup

Serves: 4 Preparation Time: 5 minutes Cooking Time: 28 minutes

Ingredients:

- Red Kidney Beans, contents of a 14 oz. can, drained and rinsed
- Bulgur Wheat, ¼ cup
- Diced Tomatoes, 1 (14 oz.) can,
- Onion, 1 whole, peeled and chopped
- Garlic, 1 clove, peeled and minced
- Basil, dried, ½ **tsp.**
- Smoked Paprika, ½ **tsp.**
- Tomato Paste, 1 **tbsp.**
- Vegetable Stock, 3 cups

Procedure:

1. Add all of the ingredients into the Soup Maker. Carefully secure the lid and set the soup maker for Smooth Soup and set the timer for 28 minutes. Once the soup has fully cooked, carefully unlatch the lid and transfer into serving bowls. Serve hot.

Nutritional Facts: Cal: 366; Carb: 76.7 g; Protein: 16.6g; Fat: 7.5g; Fiber: 19.1g; Sugars: 15.2g; Cholesterol: 0mg; Sodium: 2660mg

2.6 Carrot and Cilantro Soup

Serves: 4 Preparation Time: 10 minutes Cooking Time: 30 minutes

Ingredients:

- Cooking Spray, Low Calorie, 3 second spray
- Red Onion, 1 small piece, peeled and diced
- Potato, 1 small piece, peeled and diced
- Garlic, 1 clove, peeled and minced
- Carrots, 3 large pieces, peeled and chopped
- Coriander Seed, Ground, 1 **tbsp.**
- Vegetable Stock Cubes, 3 pieces
- Salt

- Freshly Ground Black Pepper
- Cilantro Leaves for garnish

Procedure:

1. Spray a saucepan with the cooking spray and heat over a medium flame. Sauté the onion and garlic until softened and aromatic. Add the remainder of the vegetables and cook until they have softened, about 5 minutes. Season with the ground coriander seed.
2. Transfer to the soup maker and set on a smooth setting for 30 minutes.
3. Once cooked, carefully unlatch the lid and transfer to bowls. Garnish with fresh cilantro.

Nutritional Facts: Cal: 219; Carb: 49g; Protein: 6.2g; Fat: 0.8g; Fiber: 8.3g; Sugars: 9.2g; Cholesterol: 0mg; Sodium: 221mg

2.7 Spiced Butternut Squash Soup

Serves: 4 Preparation Time: 60 minutes Cooking Time: 30 minutes

Ingredients:

- Butternut Squash, halved, seeded and scored
- Carrots, 4 medium pieces, peeled and julienned
- Garlic, 5 cloves, unpeeled
- Chili Powder, 2 pinches
- Cajun Seasoning, 1 **tsp.**
- Rosemary, Dried
- Cooking Spray, 1 second
- Salt
- Black Pepper, Freshly Ground
- Water, 3 cups
- Vegetable Stock Cubes, 2 pieces

Procedure:

1. Preheat oven to 200 degrees Celsius and prepare a baking tray. Arrange the prepared butternut squash on the tray. Remove the ends of the garlic cloves and rub all over the squash. Leave the garlic cloves within the cavity of the squash. Arrange the chopped carrots on the sides of the squash and season with the rosemary and other spices. Season with salt and black pepper. Spray the vegetables with the cooking spray and allow to roast for an hour.
2. After an hour, peel the roasted garlic cloves and add all of the ingredients into the soup maker and set for smooth for 30 minutes. Once the soup is finished cooking, transfer to serving bowls and serve hot.

Nutritional Facts: Cal: 186; Carb: 40.8g; Protein: 5.7g; Fat: 2g; Fiber: 6g; Sugars: 6.6g; Cholesterol: 0mg; Sodium: 251mg

2.8 Vegetable Soup

Serves: 4 Preparation Time: 5 minutes Cooking Time: 40 minutes

Ingredients:

- Cooking Spray, 1 second
- Leeks, 3 small pieces, rinsed and chopped
- Carrots, 2 small pieces, peeled and minced, precook by roasting or boiling
- Ginger, 2 cm piece, peeled and chopped
- Broccoli Florets, ½ cup

- Potato, 1 medium piece, peeled and chopped, precook by roasting or boiling
- Vegetable Stock Cubes, 3 pieces
- Garlic, 1 clove, crushed
- Garlic Salt, ¼ **tsp.**
- Red Chili, ½ piece
- Water, ¾ cup
- Salt
- Black Pepper, freshly ground

Procedure:

1. Add all of the ingredients into the soup maker and set to the blend setting for 40 minutes. Carefully secure the lid and allow to cook. Once the soup is done cooking, carefully unlatch the lid and transfer into serving bowls. Serve with croutons.

Nutritional Facts: Cal: 386; Carb: 88.6g; Protein: 9.6g; Fat: 2.3g; Fiber: 11.8g; Sugars: 15.8g; Cholesterol: 0mg; Sodium: 561mg

2.9 Quick Vichysoisse

Serves: 4 Preparation Time: 10 minutes Cooking Time: 40 minutes

Ingredients:

- Leeks, 2 medium sized pieces, rinsed
- Potato, 1 medium piece, peeled and chopped
- Onion, 1 piece, peeled and chopped
- Garlic, 1 clove
- Vegetable Stock, 3 cups
- Thyme Leaves, fresh
- Salt
- Black Pepper, Freshly Ground

Procedure:

1. Rinse the leeks and slice it into thin rings. Set aside. Peel and chop the potato into an even dice. Add all of the ingredients into the soup maker and set for the smooth or cream program. Secure the lid.
2. Once the soup has been fully cooked, carefully open the lid and pour into serving bowls. Serve hot or you may serve this chilled.

Nutritional Facts: Cal: 319; Carb: 72.4g; Protein: 7.6g; Fat: 6.8g; Fiber: 9.5g; Sugars: 19g; Cholesterol: 0mg; Sodium: 2366mg

2.10 Carrot Curry Soup

Serves: 4 Preparation Time: 10 minutes Cooking Time: 30 minutes

Ingredients:

- Carrot, 3 pieces, peeled
- Potato, 1 piece, peeled and chopped
- Onions, 1 piece, peeled and chopped
- Vegetable Stock, 3 cups
- Salt
- Black Pepper, freshly ground
- Curry Powder, 2 **tsp.**

- Coconut Milk, ¼ cup

Procedure:

1. Rinse the carrot and potato, and peel them. Chop them into an even dice, and add it along with the other ingredients into the Soup Maker. Secure the lid and set the smooth or cream soup setting for 30 minutes. Alternatively, you may also precook the carrots and potatoes to ensure doneness of the vegetables. Once the soup has fully cooked, carefully open the lid and pour into serving bowls.

Nutritional Facts: Cal: 381; Carb: 57.7g; Protein: 7g; Fat: 21.1g; Fiber: 10.3g; Sugars: 17.1g; Cholesterol: 0mg; Sodium: 2383mg

2.11 Creamy Tomato and Basil Soup

Serves: 4 Preparation Time: 10 minutes Cooking Time: 26 minutes

Ingredients:

- Olive Oil, 2 **tbsp.**s
- Onion, 1 cup, chopped
- Tomatoes, fresh, 2 ¼ cup
- Thyme Leaves, dried, ½ **tsp.**, crushed between fingers
- Water, 3 cups
- Basil Leaves, fresh, ¼ cup, finely chopped
- Salt
- Black Pepper, freshly ground

Procedure:

1. Heat the olive oil in a saucepan over a medium flame. Sauté the chopped onions until softened for about 4-5 minutes and transfer into the Soup Maker. Add the remainder of the ingredients and stir until well mixed.
2. Secure the lid and set for Smooth Soup for 21 minutes. Once the soup has been fully cooked, carefully lift the lid and pour into bowls to serve.

Nutritional Facts: Cal: 308; Carb: 15.4g; Protein: 2.4g; Fat: 28.4g; Fiber: 4.1g; Sugars: 7.9g; Cholesterol: 0mg; Sodium: 187mg

2.12 Hearty Celery Soup

Serves: 4 Preparation Time: 5 minutes Cooking Time: 21 minutes

Ingredients:

- Celery, 4 cups, chopped
- Onion, ½ piece, chopped
- Garlic, 2 cloves, peeled and chopped
- Vegetable Stock, 2 cups
- Salt
- Black Pepper, freshly ground
- Heavy Cream, 3 **tbsp.**s

Procedure:

1. Add all of the ingredients into the Soup Maker and secure the lid. Choose the Smooth or Cream Soup option and set the timer for 21 minutes. Once the soup has finished cooking, carefully lift the lid and pour soup into bowls. Serve hot.

Nutritional Facts: Cal: 299; Carb: 30.7g; Protein: 5.7g; Fat: 21.5g; Fiber: 8.6g; Sugars: 13g; Cholesterol: 62mg; Sodium: 1942mg

2.13 Pea Potage

Serves: 4 Preparation Time: 5 minutes Cooking Time: 21 minutes

Ingredients:

- Frozen Peas, 2 ½ cups
- Garlic, 3 cloves
- Salt, ½ **tsp.**
- Water, 2 cups

Procedure:

1. Add all of the ingredients into the Soup Maker and secure the lid. Choose the Smooth or Cream Soup option and set the timer for 21 minutes. Once the soup has finished cooking, carefully lift the lid and pour soup into bowls. Serve hot.

Nutritional Facts: Cal: 196; Carb: 37.5g; Protein: 12g; Fat: 0.7g; Fiber: 11.6g; Sugars: 9.6g; Cholesterol: 0mg; Sodium: 318mg

2.14 Spring Vegetable Soup

Serves: 4 Preparation Time: 5 minutes Cooking Time: 21 minutes

Ingredients:

- Vegetable Stock, 2 cups
- Cauliflower Florets, 8 ounces, chopped
- Asparagus, 8 ounces, chopped
- Parmesan Cheese, ¼ cup, shredded
- Nutmeg, Ground, ¼ **tsp.**
- Salt

Procedure:

1. Add all of the ingredients into the Soup Maker and secure the lid. Choose the Smooth or Cream Soup option and set the timer for 21 minutes. Once the soup has finished cooking, carefully lift the lid and pour soup into bowls. Serve hot.

Nutritional Facts: Cal: 153; Carb: 14.2g; Protein: 11.6g; Fat: 9.8g; Fiber: 4.9g; Sugars: 7.7g; Cholesterol: 14mg; Sodium: 1957mg

2.15 Creamy Summer Squash Soup

Serves: 4 Preparation Time: 10 minutes Cooking Time: 21 minutes

Ingredients:

- Zucchini, 3 medium sized pieces, cut into chunks
- Onion, 1 small piece, cut into ¼ chunks
- Garlic, 2 cloves, peeled and chopped
- Vegetable Stock, 2 cups
- Sour Cream, 4 **tbsp.**s
- Salt
- Black Pepper, freshly ground
- Lemon Juice, 1 **tbsp.**

Procedure:

1. Add all of the ingredients except the lemon juice into the Soup Maker and secure the lid. Choose the Smooth or Cream Soup option and set the timer for 21 minutes. Once the soup has finished cooking, carefully lift the lid and stir in the lemon juice. Pour soup into bowls. Serve hot.

Nutritional Facts: Cal: 275; Carb: 39.4g; Protein: 10.6g; Fat: 15.3g; Fiber: 8.4g; Sugars: 18.8g; Cholesterol: 21mg; Sodium: 1685mg

2.16 Tomato and Coconut Soup

Serves: 2 Preparation Time: 10 minutes Cooking Time: 28 minutes

Ingredients:

- Red Chili, 1 piece
- Ginger, 1 inch piece
- Onions, ¼ cup, chopped
- Tomatoes, 1 (14 oz.) can
- Coconut Milk, ¼ cup
- Desiccated Coconut, ¼ cup plus extra to garnish
- Black Pepper, freshly ground
- Salt
- Cilantro and Chili Flakes for garnish
- Water, 2 cups

Procedure:

1. Carefully remove the seeds from the chili and peel the ginger. Add all of the ingredients into the soup maker. Secure the lid and choose the cream soup setting and set the timer for 28 minutes. Once the soup is fully cooked, carefully remove the lid and pour soup into bowls. Garnish with extra desiccated coconut, a sprig of cilantro and some chili flakes before you serve it.

Nutritional Facts: Cal: 758; Carb: 36.8g; Protein: 9.4g; Fat: 69.4g; Fiber: 18.1g; Sugars: 10.2g; Cholesterol: 0mg; Sodium: 344mg

2.17 Spiced Pumpkin Potage

Serves: 3 Preparation Time: 10 minutes Cooking Time: 40 minutes

Ingredients:

- Pumpkin, 2 ½ cups
- Potato, 1 cup, cubed
- Onions, ¼ cup, chopped
- Cumin, ground, ½ **tsp.**
- Vegetable Stock, 3 cups
- Black Pepper, freshly ground
- Salt
- Feta Cheese for garnish

Procedure:

1. Halve the pumpkin and remove the seeds. There is no need to peel the pumpkin so simply cut it into evenly-sized cubes. Add the cubed pumpkin and the remainder of the ingredients into the Soup Maker. Secure the lid and program for Creamy Soup for 40 minutes.
2. Once the soup is cooked, carefully lift the lid and transfer into serving bowls. Garnish with feta cheese and serve hot.

Nutritional Facts: Cal: 179; Carb: 41.2g; Protein: 4.9g; Fat: 6.6g; Fiber: 3.9g; Sugars: 11.8g; Cholesterol: 0mg; Sodium: 2325mg

2.18 Quick Borscht

Serves: 2 Preparation Time: 10 minutes Cooking Time: 40 minutes

Ingredients:

- Beetroot, 2 cups, peeled
- Vegetable Stock, 3 cups
- Onions, ¼ cup chopped
- Sour Cream, ½ cup
- Black Pepper, freshly ground
- Salt
- Dill Weed, for garnish

Procedure:

1. Peel the beets and cut into evenly sized cubes. Add the beetroot, stock and onions into the soup maker and secure the lid. Program for Creamy or Smooth Soup and set for 40 minutes. Once the soup is ready, lift the lid and carefully stir in the sour cream. Adjust seasonings. Transfer into bowls and garnish with dill.

Nutritional Facts: Cal: 367; Carb: 31.7g; Protein: 7g; Fat: 30.5g; Fiber: 4.3g; Sugars: 21.4g; Cholesterol: 51mg; Sodium: 2509mg

2.19 Summer Corn Chowder

Serves: 3 Preparation Time: 10 minutes Cooking Time: 28 minutes

Ingredients:

- Sweet Corn, 1 can, drained
- Cream, ¼ cup
- Vegetable Stock, 2 ¾ cups
- Black Pepper, freshly ground
- Salt
- Bacon, to garnish
- Cilantro, to garnish

Procedure:

1. Add all of the ingredients except for the bacon and cilantro into the Soup Maker. Secure the lid and program for Cream Soup or Smooth, and set the timer for 28 minutes. While the soup cooks, prepare the bacon by arranging them on a skillet and rendering the fat until the bacon becomes crisp. Allow the bacon to drain on a paper towel, and crumble.
2. Once the soup has been fully cooked, transfer into bowls and garnish with the cilantro and crumbled bacon. Serve hot.

Nutritional Facts: Cal: 962; Carb: 84.1g; Protein: 39.6g; Fat: 61.9g; Fiber: 9.3g; Sugars: 19.6g; Cholesterol: 165mg; Sodium: 4958mg

2.20 Cream of Broccoli Soup

Serves: 4 Preparation Time: 10 minutes Cooking Time: 21 minutes

Ingredients:

- Vegetable Stock, 1 ½ cups
- Broccoli Florets, 16 oz.
- Salt
- Black Pepper, freshly ground
- Cheddar Cheese, 8 oz. shredded
- Heavy Cream, ½ cup

Procedure:

1. Add all of the ingredients except the cheese and cream into the Soup Maker and secure the lid. Choose the Smooth or Cream Soup option and set the timer for 21 minutes. Once the soup has finished cooking, carefully lift the lid and stir in the cheese and cream. Pour soup into bowls. Serve hot.

Nutritional Facts: Cal: 565; Carb: 10.7g; Protein: 11.5g; Fat: 56.4g; Fiber: 2g; Sugars: 5.3g; Cholesterol: 193mg; Sodium: 1476mg

2.21 Cream of Mushroom Soup

Serves: 4 Preparation Time: 10 minutes Cooking Time: 30 minutes

Ingredients:

- Unsalted Butter, 1 **tbsp.**
- Spring Onions, 1 cup, sliced
- Garlic, 1 clove, peeled and crushed
- Fresh Mushrooms, 4 cups, trimmed and sliced
- Thyme Leaves, dried, 1 **tsp.**
- Vegetable Stock, 2 ½ cups
- Salt
- Black Pepper, freshly ground
- Heavy Cream, ½ cup

Procedure:

1. In a saucepan, melt the butter over medium heat. The scallions and garlic should be cooked for about 2 minutes, or until aromatic. Cook the mushrooms for four minutes. Transfer all of the ingredients, excluding the heavy cream, to a soup maker. Stir until thoroughly mixed.
2. Secure the lid and program for Smooth or Creamy Soup and set the timer for 21 minutes. Six minutes before the timer elapses, carefully lift the lid and stir in the heavy cream. Allow the soup to finish cooking. Carefully lift the lid and transfer to bowls. Serve

Nutritional Facts: Cal: 637; Carb: 26.6g; Protein: 13.5g; Fat: 61.6g; Fiber: 5.9g; Sugars: 12.3g; Cholesterol: 194mg; Sodium: 2035mg

2.22 Chunky Cabbage Soup

Serves: 4 Preparation Time: 5 minutes Cooking Time: 28 minutes

Ingredients:

- Cabbage, 1 head, shredded
- Onion, 1 medium-sized piece, chopped
- Carrot, 1 small piece, peeled and chopped
- Garlic Cloves, 2 pieces, peeled and chopped
- Mixed Herbs, dried, 1 **tsp.**
- Salt
- Black Pepper, freshly ground
- Vegetable Stock, 3 cups

Procedure:

1. Add all of the ingredients into the soup maker. Secure the lid and program the soup maker for Chunky and set the timer for 28 minutes. Once the soup is fully cooked, carefully lift the lid and pour into bowls. Serve hot.

Nutritional Facts: Cal: 322; Carb: 73.7g; Protein: 12.6g; Fat: 7g; Fiber: 23.2g; Sugars: 38.3g; Cholesterol: 0mg; Sodium: 2488mg

2.23 Apple and Parsnip Potage

Serves: 4 Preparation Time: 5 minutes Cooking Time: 21 minutes

Ingredients:

- Parsnips, 4 pieces, peeled and chopped
- Granny Smith Apples, 2 pieces, peeled, cored and chopped
- Onion, 1 piece, peeled and chopped
- Nutmeg, Freshly ground, ½ **tsp.**
- Salt
- Black Pepper, freshly ground
- Vegetable Stock, 3 cups

Procedure:

1. Add all of the ingredients except the lemon juice into the Soup Maker and secure the lid. Choose the Smooth or Cream Soup option and set the timer for 21 minutes. Once the soup has finished cooking, carefully lift the lid and pour soup into bowls. Serve hot.

Nutritional Facts: Cal: 559; Carb: 137.3g; Protein: 6.6g; Fat: 7.8g; Fiber: 33.2g; Sugars: 66.2g; Cholesterol: 0mg; Sodium: 2362mg

2.24 Creamy Sweet Potato Soup

Serves: 4 Preparation Time: 10 minutes Cooking Time: 26 minutes

Ingredients:

- Olive Oil, 2 **tbsp.**s
- Carrots, 2 medium sized pieces, peeled and finely diced
- Onion, 1 piece, peeled and chopped
- Garlic, 2 cloves, chopped
- Salt

- Sweet Potatoes, 2 medium pieces, peeled and chopped
- Ginger, 1 inch piece, chopped
- Water, 2 ½ cups

Procedure:

1. Heat the oil in a skillet over a medium heat and sauté the carrots, onion, and garlic for 5 minutes or until softened and aromatic. Season with the salt. Add this mixture into the Soup Maker along with the other ingredients. Secure the lid and set for Smooth Soup for 21 minutes.
2. Once the soup has been fully cooked, transfer into bowls and serve hot.

Nutritional Facts: Cal: 615; Carb: 87.2g; Protein: 8.3g; Fat: 28.4g; Fiber: 14.6g; Sugars: 23.8g; Cholesterol: 0mg; Sodium: 409mg

2.25 Winter Root Vegetable Soup

Serves: 3 Preparation Time: 15 minutes Cooking Time: 21 minutes

Ingredients:

- Olive Oil, 2 **tbsp.**s
- Onion, 1 cup, peeled and chopped
- Turnips, 3 cups, peeled and chopped
- Rosemary Leaves, dried, ½ **tsp.**
- Salt
- Vegetable Stock, 3 cups
- Chives, 2 **tbsp.**s, chopped
- Black Pepper, freshly ground

Procedure:

1. Heat the oil in a medium saucepan over a medium flame and sauté the onions for 5 minutes until aromatic. Add the turnips and rosemary and season with salt. Allow to cook for 10 minutes, stirring frequently to prevent sticking. Transfer to the Soup Maker.
2. Add the remainder of the ingredients and stir to combine. Secure the lid and set for Smooth Soup for 21 minutes. Once the soup is fully cooked, transfer to serving bowls and serve immediately.

Nutritional Facts: Cal: 447; Carb: 46.7g; Protein: 5.5g; Fat: 34.7g; Fiber: 10.9g; Sugars: 27.7g; Cholesterol: 0mg; Sodium: 2583mg

2.26 British Broccoli Soup

Serves: 4 Preparation Time: 20 minutes Cooking Time: 21 minutes

Ingredients:

- Cooking Spray, 1 second
- Broccoli Florets, 2 cups
- Blue Cheese (Stilton) Triangles, 10 pieces
- Onion, 1 large piece, chopped
- Leeks, 1 stalk, chopped
- Celery, 1 stalk, chopped
- Potato, 1 medium sized piece, peeled and chopped
- Water, 3 cups
- Vegetable Stock Cubes, 2 pieces
- Thyme Leaves, dried, 2 **tsp.**

- Chili Flakes, ½ **tsp.**
- Salt
- Black Pepper, freshly ground

Procedure:
1. Spray a frying pan with the cooking spray and heat over a medium flame. Sauté the onions until softened and aromatic. Add the remainder of the vegetables and season with the spices. Cover with a lid and cook for 10 minutes. Stir occasionally.
2. Transfer the sautéed mixture to the soup maker with the remainder of the ingredients except the cheese and secure the lid. Set for smooth or creamy for 21 minutes. Once the soup has been fully cooked. Carefully lift the lid and add the cheese. Set the soup on blend for 10 minutes until well mixed. Transfer to serving bowls and serve immediately,

Nutritional Facts: Cal: 870; Carb: 70.2g; Protein: 41.6g; Fat: 51.7g; Fiber: 14.2g; Sugars: 15.2g; Cholesterol: 150mg; Sodium: 1701mg

2.27 Cheesy Cauliflower Soup

Serves: 4 Preparation Time: 10 minutes Cooking Time: 28 minutes

Ingredients:
- Cooking Spray, 1 second
- Cauliflower, 1 small head, cut into florets
- Potato, 1 large, peeled and diced
- Onion, 1 large, chopped
- Paprika, ½ **tsp.**
- Cheese, 8 triangles
- Vegetable Stock Cubes, 3 pieces
- Water, 3 cups
- Salt
- Black Pepper, freshly ground

Procedure:
1. Spray a medium skilled with the cooking spray and heat over a medium flame. Add the onions and season with paprika. Sauté until softened. Add the sautéed onion into the soup maker and add all of the other ingredients except the cheese. Secure the lid and set the soup maker for smooth or creamy for 28 minutes.
2. Once the soup has been fully cooked, carefully lift the lid and add the cheese. Set the soup maker to blend until the cheese is well incorporated. Transfer to bowls and garnish with extra paprika to serve.

Nutritional Facts: Cal: 1431; Carb: 100.8g; Protein: 76.5g; Fat: 82.9g; Fiber: 18.6g; Sugars: 17.4g; Cholesterol: 256mg; Sodium: 1800mg

2.28 Potato and Pea Curried Soup

Serves: 4 Preparation Time: 10 minutes Cooking Time: 37 minutes

Ingredients:
- Olive Oil, 1 **tbsp.**
- Onion, 1 large, peeled and chopped
- Curry Powder, 3 **tbsp.**s (adjust to taste)
- Cumin, ½ **tsp.**, ground

- Turmeric, ½ **tsp.**, ground
- Potatoes, 1 pound, peeled and chopped
- Tomatoes, 1 cup, chopped finely
- Tomato Paste, 2 **tbsp.**s
- Salt
- Black Pepper, freshly ground
- Vegetable Stock, 3 cups
- Frozen Peas, ½ cup

Procedure:

1. Heat the oil in a medium skillet over a medium heat. Sauté the onion for 3 to 4 minutes until softened. Season with the curry powder, cumin and turmeric and cook for another minute.
2. Add the potatoes to this mixture and cook for two more minutes. Transfer this mixture into the soup maker and add the remainder of the ingredients except for the peas. Stir to combine. Secure the lid and program for Chunky with the timer for 28 minutes. Six minute before the timer lapses, carefully lift the lid of the soup maker and add the peas.
3. Once fully cooked, pour into bowls and serve.

Nutritional Facts: Cal: 1642; Carb: 340.8g; Protein: 40.4g; Fat: 25.6g; Fiber: 59.8g; Sugars: 44.7g; Cholesterol: 0mg; Sodium: 2513mg

2.29 Summer Corn Chowder

Serves: 4 Preparation Time: 10 minutes Cooking Time: 28 minutes

Ingredients:

- Frozen Corn Kernels, 3 ½ cups
- Vegetable Stock, 3 cups
- Onion, ½ piece, chopped
- White Sugar, 1 **tbsp.**
- Thyme Leaves, dried, t **tsp.**
- Onion Powder, ¼ **tsp.**
- White Pepper, ground, ¼ **tsp.**
- Salt
- Cornstarch, 1 **tsp.**
- Water, 2 **tbsp.**s
- Heavy Cream, 1/3 cup

Procedure:

1. Into the container of the Soup Maker, add 2 ½ cups of the corn kernels, the stock, onions, sugar, thyme, onion powder, white pepper and salt. Secure the lid and set the Soup Maker for Chunky, for 28 minutes.
2. While the soup cooks, stir the cornstarch into the water. Six minutes before the timer elapses, carefully open the lid and stir in the cornstarch slurry and the reserved cup of corn. Once the soup has been fully cooked, lift the lid and add the heavy cream. Serve immediately.

Nutritional Facts: Cal: 651; Carb: 92.2g; Protein: 10g; Fat: 37.4g; Fiber: 9.1g; Sugars: 31.1g; Cholesterol: 109mg; Sodium: 2354mg

2.30 Pasta a Fagioli Soup

Serves: 4 Preparation Time: 5 minutes Cooking Time: 28 minutes

Ingredients:

- Paprika, 1/8 **tsp.**
- Vegetable Oil, 2 **tsp.**
- Red Pepper Flakes, ¼ **tsp.**, crushed
- Leek, 1 large stalk, chopped
- Garlic, 2 cloves, minced
- Rosemary Leaves, 1 **tsp.**, crushed
- Vegetable Stock, 3 cups
- Navy Beans, 1 can, rinsed and drained
- Tomato, 1 large, chopped
- Orzo Pasta, ½ cup
- Salt
- Black Pepper, freshly ground

Procedure:

1. Heat the oil in a medium saucepan over a medium flame. Sauté the leeks and garlic and season with the rosemary, red pepper flakes and paprika. Cook for 2 minutes.
2. Add this and the remainder of the ingredients into the Soup Maker. Stir to combine before your secure the lid. Select the Chunky Setting for the Soup Maker and set the timer for 28 minutes. Once fully cooked, carefully lift the lid and pour into bowls. Serve hot.

Nutritional Facts: Cal: 1609; Carb: 291.7g; Protein: 66.3g; Fat: 25.7g; Fiber: 16.7g; Sugars: 12g; Cholesterol: 280mg; Sodium: 3613mg

2.31 Scotch Broth

Serves: 4 Preparation Time: 10 minutes Cooking Time: 50 minutes

Ingredients:

- Vegetable Oil, 1 **tbsp.**
- Onion, 1 piece, finely chopped
- Turnips, 2 pieces, peeled and diced
- Carrots, 2 pieces, peeled and diced
- Leek, 1 piece, rinsed, trimmed and sliced
- Pearl Barley, 100 grams, washed
- Lamb Stock, 3 ½ cups
- Kale, 70 grams, midrib removed, leaves finely chopped
- Salt
- Black Pepper, freshly ground

Procedure:

1. Add the oil and set the soup maker to high for 30 minutes. Once the oil is hot, add the onions and sauté for two minutes, or until they have softened. Use the stir function periodically. Cook the turnips, carrots, and leeks for an additional 4 minutes. Stir periodically.
2. Add the spice, stock and pearl barley,. Cover and allow the soup maker to bring the contents to a boil. Utilize the stir feature. Allow to boil on high for one minute before reducing to a simmer. Two minutes before the timer elapses, inspect the pearl barley. If the kale is soft, mix it in with salt and pepper. If difficulty persists, add 10 minutes to the cycle.
3. Blend to finish the soup. Transfer into bowls and serve immediately.

Nutritional Facts: Cal: 855; Carb: 138.9g; Protein: 45g; Fat: 15.1g; Fiber: 26.7g; Sugars: 23.2g; Cholesterol: 0mg; Sodium: 3958mg

2.32 Potato Pepper Pot

Serves: 4 Preparation Time: 10 minutes Cooking Time: 30 minutes

Ingredients:

- Olive Oil, 1 **tbsp.**
- Onion, 1 large piece, peeled and chopped
- Garlic, 3 cloves, crushed
- Sweet Potatoes, 500 grams peeled and cubed
- Bell Peppers, 2 pieces, seeded and chopped
- Vegetable Stock, 3 ½ cups
- Chili Peppers, 2 pieces, seeded and chopped
- Salt
- Black Pepper, freshly ground

Procedure:

1. Heat the soup maker on high for 30 minutes and add the olive oil. Cook the onions and garlic for 1-3 minutes. Use the stir function. Add the sweet potatoes, bell peppers, vegetable stock and chili. Bring to a boil then reduce to a simmer to let the soup finish cooking, the vegetables should be soft. Blend until smooth and season with salt and pepper. Transfer into bowls and serve immediately.

Nutritional Facts: Cal: 888; Carb: 179.8g; Protein: 11.5g; Fat: 22.4g; Fiber: 26.7g; Sugars: 22.3g; Cholesterol: 0mg; Sodium: 2733mg

2.33 Mixed Vegetable Borscht

Serves: 4 Preparation Time: 10 minutes Cooking Time: 28 minutes

Ingredients:

- Beets, 2 cups, peeled and cubed
- Potato, 1 cup, peeled and cubed
- Carrot, 1 piece, peeled and diced
- Parsnip, 1 piece, peeled and diced
- Cabbage, ½ cup, shredded
- Celery, 1 small stalk, finely chopped
- Green Beans, 5 pieces, trimmed and cut into 2 inch pieces
- Onion, 1 small piece, peeled and chopped
- Salt
- Vegetable Stock, 3 cups
- Garlic, 1 clove, crushed

Procedure:

1. Add all of the ingredients into the soup maker and season with salt. Secure the lid and program for Chunky set at 28 minutes. Once the soup has been cooked, transfer into bowls and serve immediately.

Nutritional Facts: Cal: 421; Carb: 96.5g; Protein: 13.3g; Fat: 7.3g; Fiber: 25g; Sugars: 37.2g; Cholesterol: 0mg; Sodium: 2539mg

2.34 Traditional French Onion Soup

Serves: 4 Preparation Time: 5 minutes Cooking Time: 21 minutes

Ingredients:

- Onions, 3 large pieces, sliced
- Carrot, 1 small piece, peeled and finely chopped
- Garlic, 2 cloves, crushed
- Vegetable Stock, 3 cups, heated
- White Wine, 1 cup
- Salt
- Thyme Leaves, dried, ¼ **tsp.**

Procedure:

1. Add all of the ingredients into the soup maker and secure the lid. Program for Chunky set at 21 minutes. Once the soup has been fully cooked, use the blend option to puree the soup to your desired consistency. Transfer into bowls and serve immediately.

Nutritional Facts: Cal: 340; Carb: 58.8g; Protein: 5.9g; Fat: 6.6g; Fiber: 11.4g; Sugars: 28.6g; Cholesterol: 0mg; Sodium: 2375mg

2.35 Mixed Vegetable Soup

Serves: 4 Preparation Time: 10 minutes Cooking Time: 21 minutes

Ingredients:

- Potato, 1/2 cup, peeled and diced
- Parsnip, 1/2 cup, peeled and diced
- Pumpkin, 1/2 cup, diced
- Red Bell Peppers, 1 small piece, seeded and chopped
- Carrot, ½ cup, peeled and diced
- Onion, 1 small piece, peeled and diced
- Garlic, 2 cloves, minced
- Vegetable Stock, 3 ¼ cups
- Salt

Procedure:

1. Add all of the ingredients into the soup maker and season with salt. Secure the lid and program for Chunky, and time for 21 minutes. Once the soup is cooked, use the puree function and blend the soup to your desired consistency. Transfer into bowls and serve immediately.

Nutritional Facts: Cal: 222; Carb: 51g; Protein: 5.2g; Fat: 7.1g; Fiber: 9.1g; Sugars: 18.9g; Cholesterol: 0mg; Sodium: 2557mg

2.36 Gazpacho

Serves: 4 Preparation Time: 5 minutes Cooking Time: 21 minutes

Ingredients:

- Onion, 1 medium piece, peeled and minced
- Tomatoes, 3 large pieces, seeded and chopped
- Bell Pepper, 1 piece, seeded and chopped
- Celery, 2 medium stalks, chopped
- Crushed Tomatoes, 1 can, chopped

- Garlic, 2 cloves, crushed
- Vegetable Stock, 2 ½ cups, cold
- Worcestershire Sauce, a dash
- Tabasco Sauce, 2 drops

Procedure:

1. Add all of the ingredients into the soup maker and secure the lid. Program for smooth set at 21 minutes. Once the soup is done, pour into a jug and allow to chill for 30 minutes. Transfer into bowls and serve immediately. You may add pepper, feta and olive oil to garnish.

Nutritional Facts: Cal: 250; Carb: 54.7g; Protein: 9.7g; Fat: 6.9g; Fiber: 14.3g; Sugars: 29g; Cholesterol: 0mg; Sodium: 2116mg

2.37 Pumpkin Curry Soup with Dukkha

Serves: 4 Preparation Time: 10 minutes Cooking Time: 21 minutes

Ingredients:

- Pumpkin, 2 ½ cups, chopped
- Potato, 1 ½ cup, peeled and chopped
- Leek, white part only, 1 piece, rinsed and finely sliced
- Garlic, 2 cloves, crushed
- Vegetable Stock, 3 cups
- Curry Powder, 2 **tsp.**
- Dukkha for garnish
- Hummus for garnish
- Cilantro Leaves for garnish

Procedure:

1. Add all of the ingredients except for the garnishes into the soup maker and secure the lid. Program for Smooth, set at 21 minutes. Once the soup has been fully cooked, use the blender function for 15 seconds until the soup reaches your desired consistency. Transfer into bowls and garnish with the Dukkah, Hummus and Cilantro Leaves. Serve immediately.

Nutritional Facts: Cal: 418; Carb: 73.3g; Protein: 14g; Fat: 16.1g; Fiber: 12.3g; Sugars: 15.3g; Cholesterol: 0mg; Sodium: 2462mg

2.38 Creamy Mushroom Soup

Serves: 4 Preparation Time: 10 minutes Cooking Time: 21 minutes

Ingredients:

- Button Mushrooms, 2 ½ cups, sliced
- Brown Mushrooms, 2 ½ cups, sliced
- Potato, 2 cups, diced
- Leek, 1 piece, rinsed and sliced thinly
- Garlic, 2 cloves, crushed
- Vegetable Stock, 2 ½ cups, hot
- Worcestershire Sauce, 2 **tbsp.**s
- Halloumi, 200 grams, sliced

Procedure:

1. Add all of the ingredients into the soup maker except for the Halloumi. Secure the lid of the soup maker and program for smooth. Once the soup has finished cooking, use the blender

function for 15 seconds to blend until the soup is the desired consistency. Transfer into bowls and serve with the halloumi.

2. While the soup cooks, heat a non-stick skillet over a medium flame and fry the halloumi, turning once each side becomes browned. Use this to garnish the soup before it is served.

Nutritional Facts: Cal: 788; Carb: 73.9g; Protein: 45.5g; Fat: 41.2g; Fiber: 8.1g; Sugars: 21.9g; Cholesterol: 95mg; Sodium: 3581mg

2.39 Spiced Sweet Potato and Lentil Soup

Serves: 4 Preparation Time: 10 minutes Cooking Time: 21 minutes

Ingredients:

- Sweet Potato, 3 cups, peeled and diced
- Potato, 1 ½ cups, peeled and diced
- Lentils, ½ cup, cooked
- Onion, 1 medium piece, finely chopped
- Garlic, 2 cloves, crushed
- Vegetable Stock, 2 ½ cups, hot
- Coconut Cream, ¾ cup
- Salt
- Dried Cumin Seed, 2 **tsp.**, ground

Procedure:

1. Add all of the ingredients into the soup maker except for the salt and coconut cream. Secure the lid and program for smooth set for 21 minutes. Once the soup has been fully cooked, stir in the salt and coconut cream. Use the blender function of the soup maker and puree until the soup reaches your desired consistency. Transfer into bowls and serve immediately.

Nutritional Facts: Cal: 1612; Carb: 296.7g; Protein: 27.8g; Fat: 43.8g; Fiber: 32.8g; Sugars: 164.1g; Cholesterol: 0mg; Sodium: 2504mg

2.40 Sweetened Parsnip Soup

Serves: 4 Preparation Time: 10 minutes Cooking Time: 26 minutes

Ingredients:

- Olive Oil, 1 **tbsp.**
- Onion, 1 medium piece, finely chopped
- Parsnips, 2 medium pieces, peeled and finely diced
- Apples, 2 pieces, peeled, cored and diced
- Salt
- Black Pepper, freshly ground
- Honey, 2 **tbsp.**s
- Thyme Leaves, dried, 2 **tsp.**
- Vegetable Stock, 3 ½ cups

Procedure:

1. Preset the soup maker on high and set for 26 minutes. Heat the olive oil in the soup maker and add the onions, cooking for 1-3 minutes until softened. Add the parsnips, apples and honey. Season with the salt, thyme and pepper and cook, using the stir function to move the vegetables and apples in the soup maker. Add the stock and allow the soup maker to boil the

soup. Reduce heat to simmer and allow the soup to finish cooking. Use the blender function to puree the soup until smooth. Transfer into bowls and serve immediately.

Nutritional Facts: Cal: 690; Carb: 144.5g; Protein: 4.7g; Fat: 22.1g; Fiber: 26g; Sugars: 92.6g; Cholesterol: 0mg; Sodium: 2709mg

2.41 Warming Pepper Soup

Serves: 4 Preparation Time: 5 minutes Cooking Time: 21 minutes

Ingredients:

- Onion, 1 large piece, chopped
- Garlic, 2 cloves, crushed
- Bell Peppers, 2 large pieces, seeded and chopped
- Potato, 1 large piece, peeled and chopped
- Chili, 1 piece, seeded and chopped
- Vegetable Stock, 3 cups

Procedure:

1. Add all of the ingredients into the soup maker and program for smooth, set at 21 minutes. Once the soup has finished cooking, transfer into bowls and serve immediately.

Nutritional Facts: Cal: 502; Carb: 113.9g; Protein: 14g; Fat: 7.5g; Fiber: 15.5g; Sugars: 17.7g; Cholesterol: 0mg; Sodium: 2201mg

2.42 Cream of Asparagus Soup (42)

Serves: 4 Preparation Time: 10 minutes Cooking Time: 21 minutes

Ingredients:

- Asparagus, 400 grams, chopped into small pieces
- Onion, 1 medium piece, peeled and chopped
- Garlic, 1 clove, crushed
- Potato, 1 medium piece, peeled and chopped
- Celery, 2 medium stalks, chopped
- Vegetable Stock, 3 ½ cups

Procedure:

1. Add all of the ingredients into the soup maker and program for smooth, set at 21 minutes. Once the soup has finished cooking, transfer into bowls and serve immediately.

Nutritional Facts: Cal: 354; Carb: 76.1g; Protein: 16.6g; Fat: 8g; Fiber: 18.2g; Sugars: 23.2g; Cholesterol: 0mg; Sodium: 2611mg

3   BEEF

3.1   Oriental Stir-Fry Soup

Serves: 4 Preparation Time: 10 minutes Cooking Time: 30 minutes

Ingredients:

- Cooking Spray, 1 second
- Mixed Vegetables for Stir-Fry, 1 800 gram bag
- Garlic, 2 cloves, peeled and minced
- Ginger, 1 3cm piece, peeled and minced or grated
- Beef Stock Cubes, 3 pieces
- Red Pepper Flakes, 1 pinch
- Water, 1 liter
- Salt
- Black Pepper, freshly ground
- Soy Sauce

Procedure:

1. Spray a skillet with the cooking spray. Heat over a medium flame. Sauté the vegetables, ginger and garlic for 10 minutes or until softened and fragrant.
2. Add all of the ingredients into the soup maker except for the soy sauce. Program for a chunky setting and set for 30 minutes. Once the soup has been fully cooked, carefully lift the lid and stir in the soy sauce. Transfer to bowls and serve warm.

Nutritional Facts: Cal: 283; Carb: 53.3g; Protein: 11.5g; Fat: 1.3g; Fiber: 7.7g; Sugars: 13.4g; Cholesterol: 0mg; Sodium: 3318mg

3.2   Indian Pasta Soup

Serves: 4 Preparation Time: 5 minutes Cooking Time: 28 minutes

Ingredients:

- Cooked Beef, 10 oz., thinly sliced
- Small Pasta such as macaroni or orzo, 3 oz., uncooked
- Garlic, 2 cloves, peeled and crushed
- Ginger, 1 **tbsp.**, grated
- Red Curry Paste, 2 **tbsp.**
- Lemongrass, 1 stalk, rinsed and peeled.
- Kaffir Lime Leaves, 2 pieces
- Red Chili, 1 piece, deseeded
- Scallions, 2 stalks, peeled and chopped
- Coconut Milk, ½ cup
- Chicken Stock, 3 ½ cup

Procedure:

1. Add all of the ingredients into the soup maker and secure the lid. Program for a Chunky Soup for 28 minutes. Once the soup has been fully cooked, remove the lemongrass and kaffir lime leaves. Pour into bowls and serve immediately.

Nutritional Facts: Cal: 2294; Carb: 74.8g; Protein: 271.8g; Fat: 93.8g; Fiber: 5.5g; Sugars: 10.2g; Cholesterol: 760mg; Sodium: 4848mg

3.3 Creamy Beefy Mushroom Soup

Serves: 4 Preparation Time: 15 minutes Cooking Time: 28 minutes

Ingredients:

- Beef Sirloin, ½ pound, sliced thinly
- Unsalted Butter, 2 **tbsp.**s
- Onion, 1 medium piece, peeled and chopped
- Garlic, 2 cloves, minced
- Button Mushrooms, ¾ pound, brushed, trimmed and sliced thinly
- Salt
- Black Pepper, freshly ground
- Chicken Broth, 3 cups
- Heavy Cream, ½ cup
- Lemon Juice, 1 **tbsp.**

Procedure:

1. Heat the butter in a medium skillet over a medium flame. Sauté the beef for 4-5 minutes or until browned on all sides. Add the onion and garlic and cook for an additional 2-3 minutes. Add the mushrooms and allow them to cook for an additional 4 minutes, stirring to make sure they do not stick to the bottom of the pan.
2. Transfer the mixture to a soup maker and add the remaining ingredients, excluding the cream and lemon juice. Lock the cover and set the timer for 28 minutes for Chunky. Carefully remove the cover six minutes before the timer expires and whisk in the cream and lemon juice. Allow to complete cooking. Immediately pour the soup into dishes and serve.

Nutritional Facts: Cal: 2279; Carb: 45.9g; Protein: 230.1 g; Fat: 125.1g; Fiber: 3g; Sugars: 17.1g; Cholesterol: 851mg; Sodium: 1856mg

3.4 Beef Burgundy Soup

Serves: 4 Preparation Time: 10 minutes Cooking Time: 28 minutes

Ingredients:

- Stewing Beef, ½ pound, sliced thinly
- Salt
- Black Pepper, freshly ground
- Carrot, 1 piece, peeled and chopped
- Celery, 1 stalk, chopped finely
- Olive Oil, 2 **tbsp.**s
- Onion, 1 small piece, peeled and chopped
- Garlic, 2 cloves, minced
- Potatoes, 2 medium pieces, peeled and diced
- Frozen Peas, ½ cup
- Tomato Paste, 2 **tbsp.**s
- Thyme Leaves, dried, 1 **tsp.**
- Bay Leaf, 1 piece
- Dry Red Wine, ½ cup
- Beef Stock, 2 ½ cups

Procedure:

1. Season the beef with salt and pepper evenly on all sides. Heat the olive oil in a skillet over a medium flame and sear the beef for 4-5 minutes until completely browned. Add the carrots, onion, celery and garlic and cook for an additional 4-5 minutes.

2. Transfer this into the soup maker and add the remainder of the ingredients. Secure the lid and program for Chunky for 28 minutes. Once the soup has fully cooked, carefully remove the lid and discard the bay leaf. Transfer into bowls and serve immediately.

Nutritional Facts: Cal: 2097; Carb: 107.2g; Protein: 227.4 g; Fat: 72.8g; Fiber: 19.4g; Sugars: 20.2g; Cholesterol: 608mg; Sodium: 2739mg

3.5 Green Pasture Soup

Serves: 4 Preparation Time: 10 minutes Cooking Time: 28 minutes

Ingredients:

- Cooked Beef, 8 oz., thinly sliced, against the grain
- Kale Leaves, 2 cups, midrib removed, rinsed and chopped
- Onion, 1 medium piece, peeled and chopped
- Garlic, 1 clove minced
- Rosemary Leaves, 1 **tsp.**, chopped
- Beef Stock, 3 cups
- Soy Sauce, low-sodium, 1 **tbsp.**
- Lime Juice, ½ **tbsp.**
- Salt
- Black Pepper, freshly ground

Procedure:

1. Add all of the ingredients into the Soup Maker. Secure the lid and program the soup maker for Chunky and set the timer for 28 minutes. Once the soup has been fully cooked, carefully lift the lid and pour into bowls. Serve immediately,

Nutritional Facts: Cal: 1448; Carb: 29.5g; Protein: 221.3 g; Fat: 44.3g; Fiber: 5.2g; Sugars: 5.3g; Cholesterol: 608mg; Sodium: 3916mg

3.6 Beefy Pulse Soup

Serves: 4 Preparation Time: 10 minutes Cooking Time: 28 minutes

Ingredients:

- Cooked Beef, 8 oz. , thinly sliced against the grain
- Cooked Lentils or Pulses, 1 cup
- Potatoes, 2 medium pieces, peeled and diced
- Carrot, 1 medium piece, peeled and diced
- Onion, 1 medium piece, peeled and diced
- Garlic, 2 cloves, peeled and minced
- Rosemary Leaves, dried, 1 **tsp.**
- Oregano Leaves, dried, 1 **tsp.**
- Chicken Stock, 3 cups
- Salt
- Black Pepper, freshly ground
- Parsley, 2 **tbsp.**s for garnish

Procedure:

1. Add all of the ingredients except the parsley into the Soup Maker. Secure the lid and program the soup maker for Chunky and set the timer for 28 minutes. Once the soup has been fully cooked, carefully lift the lid and pour into bowls. Garnish with parslet and serve immediately,

Nutritional Facts: Cal: 1909; Carb: 130.2; Protein: 236 g; Fat: 45.7g; Fiber: 30.2g; Sugars: 18.3g; Cholesterol: 608mg; Sodium: 3427mg

3.7 Mock Bolognese Soup

Serves: 4 Preparation Time: 20 minutes Cooking Time: 28 minutes

Ingredients:

- Olive Oil, 1 **tbsp.**
- Onion, 1 whole, chopped
- Garlic, 2 cloves, crushed and minced
- Beef Mince, 8 oz.
- Italian Herb Mix, 2 **tsp.**
- Canned Tomatoes, 1 (14 oz.) can, diced
- Beef Stock, 3 cups

Procedure:

1. In a non-stick skillet, heat the olive oil over a medium flame. Sauté the onions for 3-4 minutes until softened and aromatic. Add the garlic and stir to prevent burning. Add the beef mince and cook for 8 to 10 minutes until fat has rendered. Break up whole chunks with a wooden spoon.
2. Drain the beef fat and transfer to the soup maker with the remainder of the ingredients. Secure the lid and program for Chunky with the timer set for 28 minutes. Once the soup has been fully cooked, carefully lift the lid, pour into bowls and serve immediately.

Nutritional Facts: Cal: 1538; Carb: 23.5g; Protein: 218.7g; Fat: 58.6g; Fiber: 4.9g; Sugars: 9.6g; Cholesterol: 608mg; Sodium: 2812mg

3.8 Mexican Taco Soup

Serves: 4 Preparation Time: 10 minutes Cooking Time: 28 minutes

Ingredients:

- Olive Oil, 1 **tsp.**
- Beef Mince, ½ pound
- Onion, 1 small, peeled and chopped
- Garlic, 2 cloves, minced
- Bell Pepper, 1 small piece, seeded and chopped
- Tomato, 1 piece, chopped
- Taco Seasoning, 1 **tbsp.**
- Salt
- Black Pepper, freshly ground
- Beef Stock, 2 cups
- Cream Cheese or other Mexican Cheese, 4 oz.

Procedure:

1. In a non-stick skillet over a medium flame, heat the olive oil and sauté the onions, garlic and beef for 8-10 minutes or until beef is rendered and aromatic. Drain the fat and transfer the beef

into the soup maker along with the remainder of the ingredients except for the cheese. Stir to combine well.

2. Secure the lid and program for Chunky, timed at 28 minutes. Six minutes before the timer elapses, carefully lift the lid and add the cheese. Stir to combine and allow to finish cooking. Once the soup is fully cooked, transfer into bowls and serve immediately.

Nutritional Facts: Cal: 2555; Carb: 22.7g; Protein: 185.4g; Fat: 191g; Fiber: 4.3g; Sugars: 7.6g; Cholesterol: 725mg; Sodium: 2667mg

3.9 Oriental Beef Soup

Serves: 4 Preparation Time: 10 minutes Cooking Time: 28 minutes

Ingredients:

- Beef Mince, ½ pound
- Onion, 1 small piece, peeled and chopped
- Garlic, 1 clove, minced
- Bok Choy, ¾ pound, rinsed and chopped.
- Soy-Sauce, Low-Sodium, 2 **tbsp.**s
- Chicken Stock, 3 cups
- Black Pepper, freshly ground

Procedure:

1. Heat a non-stick pan over a medium flame and cook the beef for 5 minutes. Add the onion and garlic and cook for five more minutes or until fragrant. Add this into the soup maker along with the remainder of the ingredients. Stir until well combined.
2. Secure the lid and program the soup maker for chunky, with the timer set for 28 minutes. Once the soup has been fully cooked, transfer into bowls and serve immediately.

Nutritional Facts: Cal: 2005; Carb: 27g; Protein: 175.8g; Fat: 138g; Fiber: 2.6g; Sugars: 15.5g; Cholesterol: 600mg; Sodium: 7663mg

3.10 Beefy Noodle Soup

Serves: 4 Preparation Time: 10 minutes Cooking Time: 28 minutes

Ingredients:

- Olive Oil, 1 **tbsp.**
- Bell Pepper, 1 medium piece, seeded and chopped
- Onion, 1 medium piece, peeled and chopped
- Garlic, 2 cloves, crushed
- Dried Pasta, 6 oz.
- Tomato Paste, 1 (14oz.) jar
- Beef Stock, 3 cups

Procedure:

1. Heat the oil in a medium saucepan over a medium flame. Gently sauté the bell peppers and onions for 3-4 minutes until softened. Add the garlic and sauté for 1 minute. Transfer this into the soup maker along with the other ingredients. Stir until well combined.
2. Secure the lid and program the soup maker for Chunky at 28 minutes. Once the soup has fully cooked, remove the lid and transfer to bowls. Serve immediately.

Nutritional Facts: Cal: 2756; Carb: 506.7g; Protein: 113.1g; Fat: 35.2g; Fiber: 18.7g; Sugars: 49.1g; Cholesterol: 561mg; Sodium: 2891mg

3.11 Beans con Carne Soup

Serves: 4 Preparation Time: 15 minutes Cooking Time: 28 minutes

Ingredients:

- Lean Beef Mince, 6 oz.
- Onion, 1 medium piece, peeled and chopped
- Carrot, 1 medium piece, peeled and chopped
- Garlic, 1 clove, peeled and minced
- Tomato-Vegetable Juice Cocktail, 2 cups
- Chicken Stock, 1 cup
- Basil Leaves, dried, 1 **tsp.**
- Parsley Leaves, dried, 1 **tsp.**
- Black Pepper, freshly ground
- Cannellini Beans, 1 can, drained and rinsed

Procedure:

1. Heat a non-stick skillet over a medium flame and cook the beef for 8 to 10 minutes or until fully rendered. Stir occasionally to prevent sticking. Add the onions, carrots and garlic and cook for an additional 5 minutes. Add this into the soup maker along with the other ingredients. Stir to combine.
2. Secure the lid and program the soup maker for Chunky, and set the timer for 28 minutes. Once the soup has finished cooking, carefully lift the lid and pour into bowls. Serve immediately.

Nutritional Facts: Cal: 1725; Carb: 60.2g; Protein: 140.1g; Fat: 103.2g; Fiber: 18.7g; Sugars: 25g; Cholesterol: 450mg; Sodium: 2596mg

3.12 Minestrone with Meatballs

Serves: 3 Preparation Time: 5 minutes Cooking Time: 28 minutes

Ingredients:

- Onion, 1 small, finely chopped
- Zucchini, 1 small, diced
- Carrot, 1 small piece, peeled and diced
- Green Beans, 10 pieces, cut into half inch pieces
- Garlic, 1 clove, crushed
- Canned Tomatoes, 1 can, diced
- Beef Stock, 2 2/3 cups
- Tomato Puree, 1 cup
- Salt
- Macaroni, 1 cup, cooked
- Beef Meatballs, 1 dozen
- Basil Pesto
- Parmesan Cheese

Procedure:

1. Add the onions, zucchini, carrot, beans, garlic, tomatoes and tomato puree into the soup maker. Add the beef stock and the pasta and season with salt. Secure the lid and program for chunky set at 28 minutes.

2. While the soup cooks, heat a skillet over medium flame. Add oil if needed and cook the meatballs until browned. Transfer the soup into bowls and top with the meatballs, pesto and cheese. Serve immediately.

Nutritional Facts: Cal: 4161; Carb: 209.4g; Protein: 238.2g; Fat: 279.1g; Fiber: 53.9g; Sugars: 35.8g; Cholesterol: 499mg; Sodium: 9970mg

3.13 Beef Vegetable Soup

Serves: 3 Preparation Time: 10 minutes Cooking Time: 28 minutes

Ingredients:

- Potatoes, 1 ½ cups, diced
- Carrots, ½ cup, peeled and diced
- Onion, 1 small piece, peeled and diced
- Peas, 1 cup
- Celery, 2 small stalks, finely chopped
- Canned Tomato Puree, 1 can
- Beef Stock, 2 ½ cups
- Pasta, ½ cup
- Beef, 2 oz., thinly sliced
- Salt
- Black Pepper, freshly ground

Procedure:

1. Add all of the ingredients into the soup maker and secure the lid. Program for Chunky set at 28 minutes. Once the soup has been fully cooked, lift the lid, transfer into bowls and serve immediately.

Nutritional Facts: Cal: 1663; Carb: 266.7g; Protein: 112.3g; Fat: 20.4g; Fiber: 29.4g; Sugars: 55.8g; Cholesterol: 339mg; Sodium: 2608mg

3.14 Beef and Pasta Soup (14)

Serves: 4 Preparation Time: 10 minute Cooking Time: 28 minutes

Ingredients:

- Onion, 1 whole piece, chopped
- Garlic, 2 cloves, crushed
- Bell Peppers, 1 small piece, seeded and chopped
- Tomato Puree, 2 cups
- Beef Stock, 2 cups
- Oregano Leaves, dried, 2 **tsp.**
- Dried Pasta, 1 ½ cups
- Beef Mince, 4 oz.,

Procedure:

1. Add all of the ingredients into the soup maker and stir to combine. Secure the lid and program for Chunky at 28 minutes. Once the soup is cooked, transfer into bowls and serve immediately.

Nutritional Facts: Cal: 1379; Carb: 208.6g; Protein: 97.8g; Fat: 19g; Fiber: 14.4g; Sugars: 32.5g; Cholesterol: 339mg; Sodium: 1895mg

4 LAMB

4.1 Spring Lamb Soup

Serves: 4 Preparation Time: 5 minutes Cooking Time: 28 minutes

Ingredients:

- Cooked Lamb, ½ pound, cut into even chunks
- Button Mushrooms, 8 oz., brushed, trimmed and sliced
- Onion, 1 medium piece, peeled and chopped
- Garlic, 2 cloves, minced
- Green Chile, 1 piece, seeded and chopped
- Thyme Leaves, dried, 1 **tsp.**, crushed between fingers
- Cilantro Leaves, 2 **tbsp.**s, chopped finely
- Salt
- Black Pepper, freshly ground
- Chicken Stock, 3 cups
- Lemon Juice, 1 **tbsp.**

Procedure:

1. Combine all of the ingredients into the soup maker. Stir once more before you secure the lid. Program the soup maker to chunky, and set timer for 28 minutes. Once the soup has been fully cooked, carefully lift the lid and transfer soup to bowls. Serve immediately.

Nutritional Facts: Cal: 645; Carb: 56.9g; Protein: 83g; Fat: 14.5g; Fiber: 16.1g; Sugars: 10.7g; Cholesterol: 147mg; Sodium: 2769mg

4.2 Spiced Irish Lamb Soup

Serves: 4 Preparation Time: 15 minutes Cooking Time: 28 minutes

Ingredients:

- Olive Oil, 1 **tsp.**
- Onion, 1 small piece, peeled and chopped
- Lamb Mince, ½ pound
- Garlic, 2 cloves, peeled and minced
- Black Pepper
- Salt
- Cabbage, shredded to make 2 cups
- Tomatoes, 1 cup, seeded and chopped
- Thyme Leaves, dried, ½ **tsp.**
- Oregano Leaves, dried, ½ **tsp.**
- Paprika, ½ **tsp.**
- Bay Leaf, 1 large piece or 2 small pieces
- Beef Stock, 3 ½ cups

Procedure:

1. In a non-stick saucepan, heat the olive oil over a medium flame. Sauté the onions for 3-5 minutes until fragrant. Add the lamb mince and garlic and season with the salt and pepper. Taste and adjust seasonings. Allow the lamb to cook for 10 minutes.

2. Add the cooked lamb into the soup maker along with the remainder of the ingredients. Stir until evenly combined before you secure the lid. Program the Soup Maker for Chunky and set the timer for 28 minutes.

3. Once the soup has been fully cooked, carefully lift the lid, transfer into bowls and serve immediately.

Nutritional Facts: Cal: 2811; Carb: 30.3g; Protein 167.2g; Fat: 217.8g; Fiber: 8.6g; Sugars: 12.5g; Cholesterol: 640mg; Sodium: 3454mg

4.3 Middle-Eastern Lamb Soup

Serves: 4 Preparation Time: 15 minutes Cooking Time: 28 minutes

Ingredients:

- Olive Oil, 1 **tbsp.**
- Lamb Mince, ½ pound or 8 oz.,
- Onion, 1 small piece, peeled and chopped
- Garlic, 2 cloves, peeled and chopped
- Tomato Paste, 2 **tbsp.**s
- Dried Cumin Seed, ground, ½ **tsp.**
- Coriander Seed, ground, ½ **tsp.**
- Sweet Paprika, ½ **tsp.**
- Black Pepper, freshly ground
- Salt
- Bay Leaf, 1 piece or 2 small pieces
- Parsley, 3 **tbsp.**s, chopped
- Chickpeas, canned, 1 cup, rinsed and drained
- Tomatoes, 1 cup, seeded and chopped
- Beef Stock, 3 cups

Procedure:

1. Heat a non-stick skillet over a medium flame, heat the oil. Cook the lamb mince for 8-10 minutes. Add the onions and garlic and cook for an additional 5 minutes or until aromatic and fragrant. Add the cooked lamb mixture into the soup maker and add the other ingredients. Stir to combine.

2. Secure the lid and program the soup maker for Chunky. Set the timer for 28 minutes. Once the soup has been fully cooked, carefully lift the lid and pour into bowls. Remove the bay leaf. Serve immediately.

Nutritional Facts: Cal: 3580; Carb: 148.5g; Protein 204.1g; Fat: 236.9g; Fiber: 41g; Sugars: 31.9g; Cholesterol: 640mg; Sodium: 2968mg

4.4 Mediterranean Lamb Soup (4)

Serves: 4 Preparation Time: 5 minutes Cooking Time: 28 minutes

Ingredients:

- Lamb, cooked, ¾ pound, cut into even chunks
- Long-Grain Rice, 1 cup, cooked
- Onion, 1 small, peeled and minced
- Garlic, 2 cloves, crushed
- Tomato Paste, 2 **tbsp.**s

- Water, 3 ½ cups
- Dill, 2 **tbsp.**s, chopped
- Salt

Procedure:

1. Add all of the ingredients into the soup maker except for the dill. Secure the lid and program the soup maker for Chunky and set the timer for 28 minutes. Once the soup has been fully cooked, transfer into bowls and garnish with the chopped dill. Serve immediately,

Nutritional Facts: Cal: 2655; Carb: 166.7g; Protein: 303g; Fat: 76.3g; Fiber: 5.7g; Sugars: 7.3g; Cholesterol: 918mg; Sodium: 1003mg

5 POULTRY

5.1 Chicken and Corn Soup

Serves: 2 Preparation Time: 10 minutes Cooking Time: 30 minutes

Ingredients:

- Carrot, 1 large piece, peeled and chopped
- Chicken Breast, skinless and trimmed, 1 piece
- Onion, 1 small piece, peeled and chopped
- Sweet Corn or Canned Corn Kernels, 1 can, drained
- Chicken Stock, 3 cups
- Parsley, fresh, 1 **tbsp.**, chopped plus extra for garnish
- Thyme Leaves, 6 sprigs

Procedure:

1. Peel and slice the carrot into small, even cubes. Slice the chicken breast into larger-sized cubes. Add these prepared ingredients along with the remainder of the ingredients except the extra parsley into the soup maker. Secure the lid and set the soup maker for chunky and set the time for 30 minutes. Once the soup is cooked, carefully lift the lid. Check the chicken for doneness, and if fully cooked, transfer into bowls and serve, otherwise allow to cook for an additional 5 minutes until fully cooked. Garnish with the chopped parsley.

Nutritional Facts: Cal: 337; Carb: 45.7g; Protein: 29.9g; Fat: 6.1g; Fiber: 7.9g; Sugars: 13.7g; Cholesterol: 64mg; Sodium: 2420mg

5.2 Mulligatawny

Serves: 3 Preparation Time: 15 minutes Cooking Time: 35 minutes

Ingredients:

- Ginger, fresh, 2 cm piece, peeled and minced
- Garlic, 2 cloves, peeled and minced
- Celery, 1 small stalk, finely chopped
- Carrot, 1 small piece, peeled and chopped
- Onions, 1 small piece, peeled and chopped
- Mango or Apple, 1 piece, seeded and sliced
- Chicken Breast, 1 piece, skinless and trimmed
- Long-grain Rice, ¼ cup, uncooked
- Turmeric, ground, 1 **tbsp.**
- Dried Cumin Seed, ½ **tsp.**, ground
- Chicken Stock, 3 ½ cups
- Salt
- Black Pepper, freshly ground
- Lemon Juice, 1 **tbsp.**
- Yogurt , for garnish
- Cilantro Leaves, for garnish

Procedure:

1. Peel and mince the ginger and garlic. Dice the carrot, celery and onion into even pieces. Pare the mango or apple and slice thinly. Cut the chicken into cubes. Add these and the other

ingredients except for the lemon juice, yogurt and cilantro into the Soup Maker. Secure the lid and program the soup maker for chunky. Once the soup is fully cooked, open the lid and stir in the lemon juice. Pour into bowls and garnish with a dollop of yogurt and cilantro leaves.

Nutritional Facts: Cal: 647; Carb: 114.8g; Protein: 35.5g; Fat: 7.5g; Fiber: 11g; Sugars: 56g; Cholesterol: 72mg; Sodium: 2950mg

5.3 Chicken and Mushroom Soup

Serves: 4 Preparation Time: 20 minutes Cooking Time: 21 minutes

Ingredients:

- Cooking Spray, 1 second spray
- Chicken Breasts, 2 pieces, skinned and diced
- Button Mushrooms, 2 cups, brushed, trimmed and sliced
- Onion, 1 medium piece, peeled and diced
- Garlic, 1 clove, peeled and minced
- Carrot, 1 medium piece, peeled and diced
- Celery, 1 stalk, peeled and minced
- Water, 3 cups
- Milk, ½ cup
- Worcestershire Sauce, 1 **tsp.** or a dash
- Thyme Leaves, dried, 1 **tsp.**
- Chicken Stock Cubes, 3 pieces
- Black Pepper, freshly ground
- Salt

Procedure:

1. Spray a skillet with the cooking spray and cook the chicken until golden. Reduce heat to medium and sauté the onions and garlic until softened. Add the carrots and celery and cook for 5 more minutes or until the carrots have softened. Add the sliced mushrooms and cook for 10 minutes. Add the cooked mixture into the soup maker along with the other ingredients. Program for smooth and set the timer for 21 minutes. Once the soup has been fully cooked, transfer into bowls and serve.

Nutritional Facts: Cal: 546; Carb: 35.1g; Protein: 51.4g; Fat: 22.9g; Fiber: 6.5g; Sugars: 16.2g; Cholesterol: 135mg; Sodium: 3893mg

5.4 Chicken Vichysoisse

Serves: 4 Preparation Time: 15 minutes Cooking Time: 28 minutes

Ingredients:

- Cooking Spray, 1 second
- Cooked Chicken, skinless, cut into chunks
- Potatoes, 2 medium pieces, peeled and diced
- Onion, 1 large, peeled and diced
- Leeks, white part only, 2 stalks, rinsed and sliced
- Carrot, 1 medium piece, peeled and diced
- Celery, 2 stalks, diced
- Skim Milk, ½ cup
- Thyme Leaves, dried, 1 **tsp.**

- Chicken Stock Cubes, 2 pieces
- Water, 2 ½ cups
- Black Pepper, freshly ground
- Salt
- Yogurt or Crème Fraiche for garnish

Procedure:

1. Spray a skillet with the cooking spray and sauté the onions over a medium heat, add the chicken and cook until the onions have softened. Add the vegetables and season with the thyme and seasonings. Spray with more cooking spray if necessary. Cover the vegetables and chicken with a lid and allow to cook for 10 minutes until the chicken has been cooked through.
2. Add the cooked chicken and vegetables into the soup maker and add the milk, water and chicken stock cubes and program the soup maker for smooth at 28 minutes. Once the soup has been fully cooked, transfer into bowls and garnish with the yogurt or crème fraiche. Serve immediately.

Nutritional Facts: Cal: 729; Carb: 124g; Protein: 46.8g; Fat: 5.8g; Fiber: 19.8g; Sugars: 28.3g; Cholesterol: 82mg; Sodium: 2784mg

5.5 Chicken Corn Chowder

Serves: 4 Preparation Time: 10 minutes Cooking Time: 28 minutes

Ingredients:

- Cooking Spray, 1 second
- Chicken Breasts, 2 pieces, uncooked, skinned and diced
- Potato, 1 large piece, peeled and sliced
- Milk, ½ cup
- Onion, 1 large, diced
- Celery, 1 stalk, diced
- Sweet Corn, 1 can, rinsed and drained
- Chicken Stock Cubes, 2 pieces
- Bay Leaf, 1 large piece, or 2 small pieces
- Smoked Paprika, 2 **tsp.**
- Thyme Leaves, 1 **tsp.**, dried
- Water, 3 cups
- Black Pepper, freshly ground
- Salt
- Cilantro Leaves for garnish

Procedure:

1. Spray a skillet with the cooking spray and cook the chicken over a medium heat until golden. Add the onions, garlic, and celery and sauté until softened. Add these ingredients into the soup maker and add the other ingredients except for the cilantro leaves. Secure the lid and program the soup maker for chunky, and time it for 28 minutes. Once the soup has fully cooked, remove the bay leaves and transfer into bowls. Garnish with cilantro leaves and serve immediately.
2. If the soup is too thin, pour half the soup into a bowl and use the blender function in the soup maker until the soup is smooth. Add the soup in the bowl and stir to combine.

Nutritional Facts: Cal: 864; Carb: 132g; Protein: 64.5g; Fat: 12.5g; Fiber: 18.4g; Sugars: 22.1g; Cholesterol: 130mg; Sodium: 3337mg

5.6 Oriental Chicken Soup

Serves: 4 Preparation Time: 15 minutes Cooking Time: 28 minutes

Ingredients:

- Cooking Spray, 1 second
- Chicken Meat, 2 pieces, cooked and sliced
- Thyme, fresh, 4 sprigs
- Garlic, 2 cloves, peeled and minced
- Scallions, 2 stalks, trimmed and sliced
- Shiitake Mushrooms, ½ cup, trimmed and sliced
- Ginger, 1 2-cm piece, peeled and grated
- Green Bell Pepper, 1 medium piece, seeded and chopped
- Potato, 1 medium piece, peeled and chopped
- Water, 3 cups
- Chicken Stock Cubes, 3 pieces
- Celery Salt, ½ **tsp.**
- Salt
- Black Pepper, freshly ground

Procedure:

1. Spray a large skillet with the cooking spray and heat over a medium flame. Sauté the onions, garlic, mushrooms, and ginger until they have softened and are aromatic. Add these into the soup maker with the other ingredients and program the soup maker for chunky. Set the timer for 28 minutes. Once the soup has fully cooked, lift the lid and remove half the contents of the soup. Use the blender setting on the soup maker, and blend the remainder of the soup until smooth. Add the rest of the soup and serve immediately.

Nutritional Facts: Cal: 577; Carb: 66.1g; Protein: 52.6g; Fat: 12.2g; Fiber: 9.6g; Sugars: 8g; Cholesterol: 132mg; Sodium: 3785mg

5.7 Mediterranean Chicken Soup

Serves: 4 Preparation Time: 15 minutes Cooking Time: 28 minutes

Ingredients:

- Cooking Spray, 1 second
- Onion, 1 medium piece, peeled and diced
- Garlic, 1 clove, peeled and minced
- Chicken Breasts, 1 whole piece, cubed
- Yellow Bell Pepper, 1 whole piece, seeded and diced
- Celery Stalk, 1 large piece, diced
- Tomatoes, 1 can
- Green Beans, ¼ cup, chopped
- Rosemary, dried, 1 pinch
- Chicken Stock Cubes, 2 pieces
- Water, 2 ½ cups

- Black Pepper, freshly ground
- Salt

Procedure:

1. Spray a skillet with cooking spray and fry the chicken over a medium flame until golden. Add the bell peppers, celery, onion and garlic and add the seasonings. Sauté the vegetables until the onions have softened. Add these into the soup maker along with the other ingredients. Secure the lid and program the soup maker for chunky, for 28 minutes. Once soup is fully cooked, transfer into bowls and serve immediately.

Nutritional Facts: Cal: 450; Carb: 37.3g; Protein: 49.6g; Fat: 12.4g; Fiber: 8.5g; Sugars: 5.9g; Cholesterol: 131mg; Sodium: 2797mg

5.8 Spanish Chicken Soup

Serves: 3 Preparation Time: 15 minutes Cooking Time: 21 minutes

Ingredients:

- Cooking Spray, 1 second
- Chicken Breast, 1 piece, cubed
- Red Onions, 2 medium pieces, peeled and diced
- Garlic, 1 clove, peeled and minced
- Chorizo (spicy or not spicy), 2 links, diced
- Sweet Potato, 1 medium piece, peeled and diced
- Canned Tomatoes, 1 can
- Sweet Corn, 1 can
- Water, 3 cups
- Black Pepper, freshly ground
- Salt

Procedure:

1. Spray a skillet with cooking spray and cook the chicken until golden. Add the onions, garlic and chorizo and cook until the onions have softened. Transfer this into the soup maker along with the remainder of the ingredients. Secure the lid and program for chunky, timed at 28 minutes. Once the soup is cooked, carefully lift the lid and transfer into bowls. Serve immediately.

Nutritional Facts: Cal: 1234; Carb: 138.6g; Protein: 66.6g; Fat: 51g; Fiber: 20.2g; Sugars: 34.4g; Cholesterol: 170mg; Sodium: 2847mg

5.9 Creamy Cheesy Chicken Soup

Serves: 4 Preparation Time: 5 minutes Cooking Time: 28 minutes

Ingredients:

- Butter, 1 **tbsp.**
- Tomatoes, ¼ cup, finely chopped
- Serrano Pepper, 1 piece, seeded and chopped
- Taco Seasoning, 1 **tsp.**
- Chicken Stock, 2 cups
- Cream Cheese, 4 oz., softened
- Salt
- Cooked Chicken, 8 oz., shredded
- Heavy Cream, ¼ cup

- Cilantro Leaves, 2 **tbsp.**s, for garnish

Procedure:

1. Heat the butter in a non-stick skillet, and cook the tomatoes and peppers. Season with the taco seasoning and cook for 1-2 minutes. Transfer this into a soup maker. Pour in the stock, cream cheese and salt. Layer the shredded chicken next. Secure the lid and program the soup maker for chunky. Set the timer for 28 minutes. Once the soup is cooked, carefully lift the lid and transfer into bowls. Garnish with cilantro before you serve.

Nutritional Facts: Cal: 963; Carb: 12.3g; Protein: 52.3g; Fat: 78.5g; Fiber: 0.8g; Sugars: 3.1g; Cholesterol: 344mg; Sodium: 2773mg

5.10 Southeast Asian Coconut Chicken Soup

Serves: 4 Preparation Time: 5 minutes Cooking Time: 28 minutes

Ingredients:

- Ginger, ground, 1 tsp.
- Chicken Stock, 1 ¾ cups
- Chili-Garlic Paste, 1 tbsp.
- Coconut Milk, unsweetened, 1 ¾ cups
- Lime Juice, 1 tbsp.
- Fish Sauce, 1 tbsp.
- Soy Sauce, low-sodium, 1 tbsp.
- Chicken Breasts, 2 pieces, cubed
- Basil Leaves, 2 leaves
- Parsley, fresh, 3 **tbsp.**s, chopped

Procedure:

1. Add all of the ingredients except the parsley into the soup maker. Secure the lid and program for Chunky, with timer set at 28 minutes. Once the soup is fully cooked, remove the basil and transfer into bowls. Garnish with parsley and serve immediately.

Nutritional Facts: Cal: 1547; Carb: 30.4g; Protein: 94.5g; Fat: 122.1g; Fiber: 10.2g; Sugars: 16.8g; Cholesterol: 249mg; Sodium: 4060mg

5.11 Herbed Poultry Potage

Serves: 2 Preparation Time: 5 minutes Cooking Time: 21 minutes

Ingredients:

- Olive Oil, 1 tbsp.
- Onion, 1 medium piece, chopped
- Garlic, 2 cloves, crushed
- Cooked Chicken Meat, shredded, 5.5 oz.
- Chicken Stock Cube, 1 piece
- Water, 1 ½ cups
- Tarragon, fresh, 2 tbsp.s, chopped
- Double Cream, ¾ cup

Procedure:

1. Heat the oil in a skillet over a medium flame and sauté the onions and garlic for 5 minutes or until softened and fragrant. Add these into the soup maker with the other ingredients except

the double cream. Secure the lid and program for smooth set at 21 minutes. Once the soup is cooked, lift the lid and stir in the double cream. Transfer into bowls and serve immediately.

Nutritional Facts: Cal: 1287; Carb: 23.2g; Protein: 78g; Fat: 98.8g; Fiber: 2.9g; Sugars: 5g; Cholesterol: 463mg; Sodium: 1450mg

5.12 Chili Chicken Soup

Serves: 2 Preparation Time: 5 minutes Cooking Time: 28 minutes

Ingredients:

- Cooked Chicken, shredded, ½ cup
- Onion, ½ cup, chopped
- Green Chiles, 1 14 oz. can, diced
- Tomatoes, 1 cup
- Chicken Stock, 2 cups
- Dried Cumin Seed, 1 tsp.
- Coriander Seed, ½ tsp.
- Heavy Cream, ¼ cup
- Garlic, 2 cloves, peeled and minced
- Jalapeno, 1 seeded and chopped
- Salt

Procedure:

1. Add all of the ingredients into the soup maker. Secure the lid and program for Chunky, with timer set at 28 minutes. Once the soup is fully cooked, transfer into bowls and serve immediately.

Nutritional Facts: Cal: 471; Carb: 32.3g; Protein: 26.5g; Fat: 26.6g; Fiber: 5.4 g; Sugars: 10.2g; Cholesterol: 135mg; Sodium: 2917mg

5.13 Chunky Chicken Salsa Sopas

Serves: 4 Preparation Time: 5 minutes Cooking Time: 28 minutes

Ingredients:

- Chicken Thighs, deboned and skinned, 8 oz., thinly sliced
- Chicken Stock, 3 cups
- Enchilada Sauce, 4 oz.,
- Salsa Verde, 2 oz.,
- Salt
- Black Pepper, freshly ground
- Monterey Jack, ¼ cup, shredded
- Heavy Cream, ¼ cup

Procedure:

1. Add all of the ingredients into the soup maker except for the cheese and heavy cream. Secure the lid and program for Chunky, with timer set at 28 minutes. Six minutes before the timer elapses, open the lid and stir in the cheese and heavy cream. Once the soup is fully cooked, transfer into bowls and serve immediately.

Nutritional Facts: Cal: 2315; Carb: 23.4g; Protein: 173.9g; Fat: 172.1g; Fiber: 1.5g; Sugars: 8.7g; Cholesterol: 23.4mg; Sodium: 6935mg

5.14 Cream Chicken Potato Potage

Serves: 4 Preparation Time: 5 minutes Cooking Time: 21 minutes

Ingredients:

- Cooked Chicken, 7 oz., shredded
- Garlic, 2 cloves, crushed
- Onion, 1 medium piece, peeled and chopped
- Potatoes, 7 oz., cleaned, peeled and chopped
- Chicken Broth, 2 cups
- Crème Fraiche, 2 **tbsp.**s

Procedure:

1. Add all of the ingredients into the soup maker except for the crème fraiche. Secure the lid and program for Smooth, with timer set at 21 minutes. Once the soup is fully cooked, lift the lid and stir in the crème fraiche. Transfer into bowls and serve immediately.

Nutritional Facts: Cal: 412; Carb: 31.3g; Protein: 42.8g; Fat: 12.1g; Fiber: 4.5g; Sugars: 7.1g; Cholesterol: 89mg; Sodium: 1619mg

5.15 Chicken and Root Vegetable Soup

Serves: 4 Preparation Time: 5 minutes Cooking Time: 28 minutes

Ingredients:

- Chicken Breast, boneless and skinless, 8 oz., cubed
- Salt
- Black Pepper, freshly ground
- Potatoes, 3 medium pieces, chopped
- Celery, 2 stalks, chopped
- Carrot, 1 large piece, peeled and chopped
- Onion, 1 medium piece, peeled and chopped
- Skim Milk, 1 cup
- Thyme Leaves, dried, 1 **tsp.**
- Tarragon Leaves, dried, 1 **tsp.**
- Chicken Stock, 2 ¼ cups
- Yogurt, 1 **tbsp.**

Procedure:

1. Season the chicken with salt and pepper. Coat evenly. Add all of the ingredients into the soup maker except for the yogurt. Secure the lid and program for Chunky, with timer set at 28 minutes. Once the soup is fully cooked, lift the lid and stir in the yogurt. Transfer into bowls and serve immediately.

Nutritional Facts: Cal: 1744; Carb: 142.6g; Protein: 219.1g; Fat: 25.9g; Fiber: 21.2g; Sugars: 38g; Cholesterol: 585mg; Sodium: 2525mg

5.16 Chicken and Summer Squash Soup

Serves: 4 Preparation Time: 5 minutes Cooking Time: 28 minutes

Ingredients:

- Coconut Oil, 1 **tbsp.**
- Carrot, 1 small piece, peeled and chopped

- Onion, 1 small piece, peeled and chopped
- Celery, 1 small stalk, chopped
- Thyme Leaves, fresh, 1 **tsp.**
- Rosemary Leaves, fresh, 1 **tsp.**
- Dried Cumin Seed, ground, ½ **tsp.**
- Chicken Stock, 4 cups
- Cooked Chicken, 1 ¼ cups
- Zucchini, 1 ¼ cups, peeled and chopped
- Salt
- Black Pepper, freshly ground
- Lime Juice, 1 **tbsp.**

Procedure:

1. Carrots, celery, and onions are sautéed in a skillet with coconut oil over medium heat for four minutes, or until tender and aromatic. Season with herbs and spices and simmer for a further minute. Transfer the seasoned mirepoix to a soup maker and add the remaining ingredients with the exception of the lime juice. Adjust the soup maker to the Chunky setting and set the timer to 28 minutes. Once the soup has reached the desired consistency, remove the cover and whisk in the lime juice. Immediately transfer to bowls and serve.

Nutritional Facts: Cal: 513; Carb: 24.6g; Protein: 57.1g; Fat: 21.8g; Fiber: 5.3g; Sugars: 11.9g; Cholesterol: 135mg; Sodium: 3390mg

5.17 Cauliflower Chicken Cream Soup

Serves: 4 Preparation Time: 5 minutes Cooking Time: 28 minutes

Ingredients:

- Unsalted Butter, 1 **tbsp.**
- Carrot, 1 medium piece, peeled and chopped
- Celery, 1 medium stalk, chopped
- Onion, ½ cup, chopped
- Garlic, 1 clove, peeled and minced
- Cauliflower, 1 head, chopped
- Cooked Chicken, 1 cup, chopped
- Parsley Leaves, dried, 1 **tsp.**, crushed
- Salt
- Black pepper, freshly ground
- Chicken Stock, 3 cups
- Heavy Cream, ½ cup
- Fresh Parsley for garnish

Procedure:

1. Heat the butter in a pan over a medium flame and sauté the onions, carrots and celery for 4 minutes until softened and aromatic. Add the garlic and cook for another minute. Transfer the mirepoix into the Soup Maker and add the remainder of the ingredients except for the fresh parsley. Secure the lid and set the soup maker for Chunky, programmed for 28 minutes. Once the soup has been fully cooked, transfer into bowls and garnish with the parsley. Serve immediately.

Nutritional Facts: Cal: 966; Carb: 52g; Protein: 58.5g; Fat: 62.3g; Fiber: 18.5g; Sugars: 23.1g; Cholesterol: 301mg; Sodium: 2914mg

5.18 Spring Chicken Soup

Serves: 4 Preparation Time: 5 minutes Cooking Time: 28 minutes

Ingredients:

- Cooked Chicken, 4 oz., shredded
- Frozen Peas, 3 ½ oz. thawed
- Onion, 1 medium piece, peeled and chopped
- Carrot, 1 large piece, peeled and chopped
- Thyme Leaves, fresh, 1 sprig, roughly chopped
- Chicken Stock, 2 cups
- Salt
- Black Pepper, freshly ground
- Lemon Juice, freshly squeezed, 1 **tsp.**

Procedure:

1. Add all of the ingredients into the soup maker except for the lemon juice. Secure the lid and program for chunky. Set the timer for 28 minutes. Once the soup has been fully cooked, stir in the lemon juice and transfer into serving bowls. Serve immediately.

Nutritional Facts: Cal: 443; Carb: 32.5g; Protein: 48.9g; Fat: 12.6g; Fiber: 8.7g; Sugars: 14.9g; Cholesterol: 118mg; Sodium: 1889mg

5.19 Winter Chicken Soup

Serves: 4 Preparation Time: 5 minutes Cooking Time: 28 minutes

Ingredients:

- Chicken Stock, 2 ½ cups
- Condensed Cream of Chicken Soup, 1 (10 ¾ oz.) can
- Cooked Chicken, 1 cup
- Frozen Mixed Vegetables, 1 cup, thawed
- Thyme Leaves, dried, ½ **tsp.**

Procedure:

1. Add all of the ingredients into the soup maker. Secure the lid and program for chunky. Set the timer for 28 minutes. Once the soup has been fully cooked, carefully lift the lid and transfer into serving bowls. Serve immediately.

Nutritional Facts: Cal: 581; Carb: 36.6g; Protein: 53.3g; Fat: 23.7g; Fiber: 4.8g; Sugars: 4.6g; Cholesterol: 132mg; Sodium: 4425mg

5.20 Southwestern Chicken Soup

Serves: 4 Preparation Time: 5 minutes Cooking Time: 28 minutes

Ingredients:

- Frozen chicken breast, 10 oz, thawed and cubed
- Carrots, 2 medium pieces, peeled and diced
- Onion, ½ large piece, peeled and diced
- Garlic. 3 cloves, peeled and minced
- Fire-Roasted Tomatoes, 1 (14 ½ oz.) can

- Black Beans, canned, ½ cup, rinsed and drained
- Corn Kernels, ½ cup
- Jalapeno Pepper. 1 piece, seeded and chopped
- Dried Cumin Seed, ground, 1 **tsp.**
- Smoked Paprika, ½ **tsp.**
- Red Chili Powder, ¼ **tsp.**
- Salt
- Black Pepper, freshly ground
- Chicken Stock, 2 cups
- Cilantro, 2 **tbsp.**s

Procedure:

1. Add all of the ingredients into the soup maker except for the cilantro. Secure the lid and program for chunky. Set the timer for 28 minutes. Once the soup has been fully cooked, carefully lift the lid and transfer into serving bowls. Garnish with cilantro and serve immediately.

Nutritional Facts: Cal: 903; Carb: 116.5g; Protein: 96.4g; Fat: 8.5g; Fiber: 26.1g; Sugars: 20g; Cholesterol: 165mg; Sodium: 2371mg

5.21 Southeast Asian Chicken Mushroom Soup

Serves: 4 Preparation Time: 25 minutes Cooking Time: 28 minutes

Ingredients:

- Chicken Stock, 4 cups
- Lemongrass, 1 stalk, crushed and sliced
- Kaffir Lime Leaves, 4 leaves
- Ginger, fresh, 1 inch piece, peeled and grated
- Salt
- Chicken Thighs, deboned and skinned, 8 oz., chopped bite-sized
- Mixed Mushrooms, 8 oz., trimmed, brushed and sliced
- Heavy Cream, ½ cup
- Cilantro, 2 **tbsp.**s

Procedure:

1. In a stockpot, add the stock, lemongrass, kaffir lime leaves and ginger. Bring to a boil over a medium flame. Season with salt and adjust to taste. Once it reaches a full rolling boil, reduce heat to low and allow to simmer for 20 minutes.
2. Remove from the heat and strain. Add this broth along with the other ingredients except for the heavy cream and cilantro into the soup maker. Program for Chunky and set the timer for 28 minutes. Six minutes before the timer elapses, lift the lid and stir in the heavy cream. Allow the soup to finish cooking and transfer into bowls. Garnish with the cilantro and serve immediately.

Nutritional Facts: Cal: 733; Carb: 24.8g; Protein: 28.6g; Fat: 59.9g; Fiber: 2.2g; Sugars: 3.7g; Cholesterol: 239mg; Sodium: 3425mg

5.22 Asian Chicken Noodle Soup

Serves: 4 Preparation Time: 5 minutes Cooking Time: 28 minutes

Ingredients:

- Chicken Breast, boneless, skinless, 8 oz., finely sliced
- Red Curry Paste, 3 **tsp.**
- Ginger, fresh, 1 **tbsp.**, grated
- Coconut Milk, unsweetened, 14 oz.,
- Chicken Stock, 2 cups
- Brown Sugar, 2 **tsp.**
- Fish Sauce, 2 **tsp.** (adjust as needed)
- Green Beans, trimmed and chopped, 1/3 cup
- Broccoli, ½ cup, rinsed and chopped
- Bok Choy, ½ cup, sliced
- Lime Juice, 2 **tbsp.**s
- Rice Noodles, 4 oz.,

Procedure:

1. Add the chicken pieces, curry paste, ginger, coconut milk, chicken stock, brown sugar and fish sauce into the soup maker and program for chunky, and set the timer for 28 minutes. After ten minutes, carefully lift the lid and add the vegetables. Allow the soup to finish cooking. Lift the lid and stir in the lime juice.
2. Arrange the noodles in the serving bowls. Top the bowls with the soup and cover for 5 minutes to cook the noodles. Serve immediately.

Nutritional Facts: Cal: 3076; Carb: 234.7g; Protein: 217.3g; Fat: 142.7g; Fiber: 21.4g; Sugars: 28.6g; Cholesterol: 573mg; Sodium: 3574mg

5.23 Hearty Chicken and Potato Egg Noodle Soup

Serves: 4 Preparation Time: 5 minutes Cooking Time: 28 minutes

Ingredients:

- Cooked chicken, 8 oz., shredded
- Potatoes, 7 oz., peeled and cubed
- Carrot, 1 small, peeled and chopped
- Garlic, 3 cloves, peeled and minced
- Lemon Juice, 2 **tbsp.**s
- Egg Noodles, 6 oz., broken
- Chicken Stock, 4 cups
- Salt
- Black Pepper, freshly ground

Procedure:

1. Add all of the ingredients into the soup maker. Secure the lid and program for chunky. Set the timer for 28 minutes. Once the soup has been fully cooked, carefully lift the lid and transfer into serving bowls. Serve immediately.

Nutritional Facts: Cal: 2072; Carb: 285.2g; Protein: 139.3g; Fat: 39.5g; Fiber: 16.8g; Sugars: 15.2g; Cholesterol: 522mg; Sodium: 3529mg

5.24 Levantine Chicken Soup

Serves: 4 Preparation Time: 5 minutes Cooking Time: 28 minutes

Ingredients:

- Chicken Breast, deboned and skinned, 8 oz., chopped

- Couscous, 1 cup
- Onion, 1 large piece, peeled and chopped
- Red Bell Pepper, 1 piece, seeded and chopped
- Chives, 2 **tbsp.**s
- Garlic Paste, 1 **tbsp.**
- Lemon Juice, 1 **tbsp.**
- Water, 3 cups
- Salt
- Black pepper, freshly ground
- Feta Cheese, ¼ cup
- Greek Yogurt, plain, 3 **tbsp.**s

Procedure:

1. Add all of the ingredients into the soup maker except for the feta and yogurt. Secure the lid and program for chunky. Set the timer for 28 minutes. Once the soup has been fully cooked, carefully lift the lid and stir in the feta cheese and yogurt. Transfer into serving bowls. Serve immediately.

Nutritional Facts: Cal: 2065; Carb: 170.2g; Protein: 241.3g; Fat: 39.3g; Fiber: 13.8g; Sugars: 16.6g; Cholesterol: 617mg; Sodium: 1225mg

5.25 Herbed Chicken Noodle Soup

Serves: 4 Preparation Time: 5 minutes Cooking Time: 28 minutes

Ingredients:

- Chicken Broth, 3 ½ cups
- Celery, ¾ cup, chopped
- Carrot, ¾ cup, peeled and chopped
- Onion, ½ cup, peeled and chopped
- Olive Oil, 1 **tbsp.**
- Thyme Leaves, dried, ½ **tsp.**
- Rosemary Leaves, dried, ½ **tsp.**
- Salt
- Black Pepper, freshly ground
- Cooked Chicken, 1 cup, shredded
- Cooked Rotini Pasta, 8 ½ oz.,
- Fresh Parsley 2 **tbsp.**s

Procedure:

1. Add all of the ingredients into the soup maker except for the parsley, pasta and chicken pieces. Secure the lid and program the soup maker for Chunky. Set the timer for 28 minutes. Six minutes before the timer elapses, lift the lid and stir in the cooked chicken and pasta. Allow the soup to finish cooking. Once it is cooked, lift the lid and transfer into bowls. Garnish with parsley and serve immediately.

Nutritional Facts: Cal: 1981; Carb: 294.8g; Protein: 116.1g; Fat: 34.9g; Fiber: 6g; Sugars: 11.6g; Cholesterol: 467mg; Sodium: 3115mg

5.26 Japanese-Style Chicken Noodle Soup

Serves: 4 Preparation Time: 10 minutes Cooking Time: 20 minutes

Ingredients:

- Chicken, 350 grams, sliced thinly
- Miso Paste, 3 **tbsp.**s
- Ginger, fresh, 3 **tsp.**, grated
- Chicken Stock, 2 ½ cups
- Scallions, 3 pieces, peeled and chopped
- Egg Noodles, 2 packs of 150 grams,
- Baby Spinach, 100 grams, washed

Procedure:

1. Set the soup maker on simmer for 20 minutes. Add the ginger, miso, chicken, chicken stock and scallions into the soup maker. Secure the lid and cook for 20 minutes. Add the noodles and allow to cook for 3-4 minutes. Stir in the spinach and allow to finish cooking for 1-2 minutes. Transfer into bowls and serve immediately. Sprinkle with soy sauce.

Nutritional Facts: Cal: 1981; Carb: 294.8g; Protein: 116.1g; Fat: 34.9g; Fiber: 6g; Sugars: 11.6g; Cholesterol: 467mg; Sodium: 3115mg

5.27 Cream of Chicken Soup

Serves: 4 Preparation Time: 10 minutes Cooking Time: 25 minutes

Ingredients:

- Butter, 1 pat
- Peanut Oil, 1 **tbsp.**
- Chicken Breast, 100 grams, sliced thinly
- Garlic, 2 cloves, crushed
- Onion, 1 small piece, chopped finely
- Leeks, 1 piece, rinsed, trimmed and chopped
- Carrots, 2 medium pieces, peeled and chopped
- Potato, 1 medium piece, peeled and cubed
- Thyme Leaves, 3 sprigs, finely chopped
- Chicken Stock, 3 cups
- Double Cream, ½ cup

Procedure:

1. Set the soup maker on high for 25 minutes and add the peanut oil and butter to the soup maker to heat up. Add the sliced chicken breast and cook for 2-3 minutes and add the onions and garlic. Let cook for 1-3 minutes. Use the stir function of the soup maker. Add the leeks and carrots and allow to cook for 2 minutes. Add the potatoes, stock and thyme. Cover and allow the soup to boil before you reduce the heat in the soup maker to simmer.
2. Use the blender function to smoothen the soup. Stir in the cream and adjust the seasonings. Cook for 2 more minutes. Transfer into bowls and serve immediately.

Nutritional Facts: Cal: 1017; Carb: 76.4g; Protein: 33.7g; Fat: 66.4g; Fiber: 11.3g; Sugars: 16.4g; Cholesterol: 238mg; Sodium: 2535mg

5.28 Turkey and Potato Soup

Serves: 4 Preparation Time: 15 minutes Cooking Time: 28 minutes

Ingredients:

- Olive Oil, 1 **tbsp.**

- Onion, ½ cup, chopped
- Carrots, ½ cup, peeled and chopped
- Celery, ½ cup, chopped
- Garlic, 2 cloves, peeled and minced
- Ground Turkey, 8 oz.,
- Tomatoes, 1 cup, finely chopped
- Chili Powder, 1 **tsp.**
- Potatoes, ¾ cup, cubed
- Sweet Potato, ¾ cup, cubed
- Chicken Broth, 4 cups
- Salt
- Black Pepper, freshly ground

Procedure:

1. Heat the olive oil in a skillet over a medium flame and sauté the onions, carrots and celery for 3-4 minutes until softened. Add the garlic and cook for another minute. Add the ground turkey and cook for 7-8 minutes until browned. Add the tomatoes and season with the chili powder and cook for 4 more minutes. Transfer this into the soup maker.
2. Add the remainder of the ingredients and secure the lid. Program for Chunky set at 28 minutes. Once the soup is cooked, transfer into bowls and serve immediately.

Nutritional Facts: Cal: 1560; Carb: 68.3g; Protein: 238.4g; Fat: 38.2g; Fiber: 13.6g; Sugars: 25.3g; Cholesterol: 496mg; Sodium: 3844mg

5.29 Wild Rice and Turkey Soup

Serves: 4 Preparation Time: 5 minutes Cooking Time: 28 minutes

Ingredients:

- Turkey Meat, 1 cup
- Carrots, ½ cup, sliced
- Onion, ½ cup, chopped
- Celery, ½ cup, chopped
- Garlic, 1 clove, minced
- Bay Leaf, 1 leaf or 2 small leaves
- Marjoram Leaves, dried, 1 **tsp.**, crushed
- Thyme Leaves, dried, 1 **tsp.**, crushed
- Garlic Powder, 1 **tsp.**
- Salt
- Black Pepper, freshly ground
- Chicken Stock, 3 cups
- Wild Rice, 1 cup, cooked
- Half and Half, ½ cup
- Parsley Leaves, fresh, 2 **tbsp.**s

Procedure:

1. Add all of the ingredients into the soup maker except for the half and half and parsley. Secure the lid and program for Chunky, set for 28 minutes. Six minutes before the timer elapses, lift

the lid and stir in the half and half. Let the soup finish cooking before it is transferred into bowls to serve. Garnish with parsley and serve immediately.

Nutritional Facts: Cal: 672; Carb: 61.1g; Protein: 55.8g; Fat: 23.5g; Fiber: 8.1g; Sugars: 11.4g; Cholesterol: 151mg; Sodium: 2691mg

5.30 Roast Chicken Soup (30)

Serves: 2 Preparation Time: 5 minutes Cooking Time: 30 minutes

Ingredients:

- Onion, 1 cup, chopped
- Carrot, 1 large piece, chopped
- Thyme Leaves, fresh, ½ **tbsp.**, chopped
- Chicken Stock, 3 cups
- Frozen Peas, 100 grams, thawed
- Roast Chicken, leftovers, 150 grams, skinned and shredded
- Greek Yogurt, 1 ½ **tbsp.**s
- Garlic, 1 clove, minced
- Lemon Juice

Procedure:

1. Add the carrot, onion, thyme, stock and peas into the soup maker and program the soup maker for chunky, set for 28 minutes. Once the soup is cooked, add the roast chicken and allow it to heat through. In a separate bowls, add the yogurt, garlic and lemon juice and stir together. Transfer the soup into bowls and stir in the yogurt mixture.

Nutritional Facts: Cal: 155; Carb: 8g; Protein: 17g; Fat: 5g; Fiber: 4g; Sugars: 6g; Cholesterol: 2mg; Sodium: 1.11mg

6 PORK

6.1 Pork and Barley Soup

Serves: 4 Preparation Time: 5 minutes Cooking Time: 28 minutes

Ingredients:

- Cooked Pork, 8 oz, cut into bite-sized cubes
- Cooked Barley, 1 cup
- Carrot, 1 medium piece, peeled and chopped
- Celery, 1 medium stalk, chopped
- Onion, 1 medium piece, peeled and chopped
- Tomato Paste, 1 **tbsp.**
- Thyme Leaves, fresh, 1 **tbsp.**, chopped
- Beef Stock, 4 cups
- Salt
- Black Pepper, freshly ground
- Lemon Juice, 2 **tsp.**

Procedure:

1. Add all of the ingredients into the soup maker except for the lemon juice. Secure the lid and program for Chunky. Set the timer for 28 minutes. Once the soup has fully cooked, lift the lid and stir in the lemon juice. Transfer into bowls and serve immediately.

Nutritional Facts: Cal: 1786; Carb: 157.8g; Protein: 214.7g; Fat: 30.6g; Fiber: 37.4g; Sugars: 13.1g; Cholesterol: 496mg; Sodium: 3789mg

6.2 Potato Pork Potage

Serves: 4 Preparation Time: 5 minutes Cooking Time: 28 minutes

Ingredients:

- Cooked Pork Meat, 8 oz., cut into bite-sized cubes
- Potatoes, 2 pieces, peeled and cubed
- Celery, 1 medium stalk, chopped
- Onion, 1 medium piece, peeled and chopped
- Bay Leaf, 1 piece
- Oregano Leaves, dried, 1 **tsp.**
- Paprika, 1 **tsp.**
- Garlic Powder, 1 **tsp.**
- Salt
- Black Pepper, freshly ground
- Chicken Stock, 3 cups
- Soy Sauce, low-sodium, 2 **tbsp.**s

Procedure:

1. Add all of the ingredients into the soup maker. Secure the lid and program for Chunky. Set the timer for 28 minutes. Once the soup has fully cooked, lift the lid and transfer into bowls. Serve immediately.

Nutritional Facts: Cal: 1384; Carb: 87.6g; Protein: 191.6g; Fat: 26.6g; Fiber: 15.1g; Sugars: 13.7g; Cholesterol: 496mg; Sodium: 4702mg

6.3 Pork and Mushroom Soup

Serves: 4 Preparation Time: 5 minutes Cooking Time: 28 minutes

Ingredients:

- Cooked Pork, 8 oz., cut into bite-sized pieces
- Button Mushrooms, ½ cup, thinly sliced
- Garlic, 2 cloves, peeled and minced
- Cabbage, 1 cup, finely sliced
- Dry Sherry, 1 **tbsp.**
- Soy-Sauce, Low-sodium, 2 **tbsp.**s
- Fresh Ginger, 1 **tsp.**, grated
- Red Pepper Flakes, ¼ **tsp.**, crushed
- Chicken Stock, 3 cups

Procedure:

1. Add all of the ingredients into the soup maker. Secure the lid and program for Chunky. Set the timer for 28 minutes. Once the soup has fully cooked, lift the lid and transfer into bowls. Serve immediately.

Nutritional Facts: Cal: 1138; Carb: 17.1g; Protein: 185.2g; Fat: 25.9g; Fiber: 2.6g; Sugars: 7.2g; Cholesterol: 496mg; Sodium: 3217mg

6.4 Pork and Lentil Soup

Serves; 4 Preparation Time: 5 minutes Cooking Time: 28 minutes

Ingredients:

- Cooked Pork, 8 oz., cut into bite-sized pieces
- Lentils, canned, 1 cup, rinsed and drained
- Onion, ½ cup, chopped
- Celery, 1 medium stalk, chopped
- Carrot, ½ cup, chopped
- Garlic, 3 cloves, minced
- Italian Seasoning, ½ **tsp.**
- Salt
- Chicken Broth, 3 ½ cups

Procedure:

1. Add all of the ingredients into the soup maker. Secure the lid and program for Chunky. Set the timer for 28 minutes. Once the soup has fully cooked, lift the lid and transfer into bowls. Serve immediately.

Nutritional Facts: Cal: 1431; Carb: 64.6g; Protein: 215.7g; Fat: 29.7g; Fiber: 19.7g; Sugars: 13.3g; Cholesterol: 496mg; Sodium: 3755mg

6.5 Green Pork and Beans Soup

Serves: 4 Preparation Time: 5 minutes Cooking Time: 28 minutes

Ingredients:

- Olive oil, 1 **tbsp.**
- Ground Pork, 8 oz.,
- Carrot, 1 medium piece, peeled and chopped

- Celery, 1 medium stalk, chopped
- Onion, 1 medium piece, peeled and chopped
- Garlic, 2 cloves, peeled and chopped
- Canned Beans, ¾ cup, rinsed and drained
- Canned Tomatoes, ½ cup
- Oregano Leaves, dried, ½ **tsp.**
- Thyme Leaves, dried, ½ **tsp.**
- Bay Leaf, 1 piece
- Salt
- Black Pepper, freshly ground
- Chicken Stock, 3 ½ cups
- Spinach Leaves, 2 cups, chopped

Procedure:

1. Heat the olive oil in a skillet over a medium flame. Sauté the ground pork for 4-5 minutes. Add in the onions, carrots and celery and cook for an additional 4 minutes or until softened and aromatic. Add the garlic and cook for another minute. Add this mixture into the soup maker with the remainder of the ingredients except the spinach. Secure the lid of the soup maker and set it for Chunky, timed at 28 minutes. Ten minutes before the timer elapses, add the spinach. Once the soup has been cooked, remove the bay leaf, transfer into bowls and serve immediately.

Nutritional Facts: Cal: 1696; Carb: 69.1g; Protein: 95.8g; Fat: 114.7g; Fiber: 18.7g; Sugars: 14g; Cholesterol: 320mg; Sodium: 3927mg

6.6 Oriental Pork Soup

Serves: 4 Preparation Time: 5 minutes Cooking Time: 28 minutes

Ingredients:

- Olive Oil, 1 **tbsp.**
- Ground Pork, 4 oz., lean
- Garlic, 1 clove, minced
- Firm Tofu, 6 oz., pressed (place the tofu on a plate and cover it with a paper towel. Add a plate on top to weigh it down), and cubed
- Chicken Stock, 2 cups
- White Pepper, ground
- Scallions, 4 **tbsp.**s

Procedure:

1. Heat the olive oil in a skillet over a medium flame and sauté the ground pork for 8 to 9 minutes. Add the garlic and cook for another minute until fragrant. Transfer this into the soup maker along with the remainder of the ingredients except for the scallions. Secure the lid and program the soup maker for chunky, timed for 28 minutes. Once the soup is cooked, lift the lid and stir in the scallions. Transfer into bowls and serve immediately.

Nutritional Facts: Cal: 1409; Carb: 5.6g; Protein: 84.6g; Fat: 114.6g; Fiber: 1.4g; Sugars: 2.5g; Cholesterol: 320mg; Sodium: 1802mg

6.7 Avocado Bacon Soup

Serves: 4 Preparation Time: 5 minutes Cooking Time: 21 minutes

Ingredients:

- Chicken Stock, 3 cups
- Avocadoes, 2 small fruits, peeled, pitted and chopped
- Cilantro, ¼ cup, roughly chopped
- Garlic, ½ **tsp.**, roughly chopped
- Lime Juice, 1 **tsp.**
- Cooked Bacon, 8 oz. chopped
- Salt
- Black Pepper, freshly ground

Procedure:

1. Add the chicken stock, avocado, cilantro, garlic and lime juice into the soup maker. Secure the lid and program the soup maker on smooth. Set the timer for 21 minutes. Once the soup is cooked, lift the lid and stir in the bacon and seasonings. Transfer into bowls and serve immediately.

Nutritional Facts: Cal: 240; Carb: 10.9g; Protein: 11.3g; Fat: 18.7g; Fiber: 2.2g; Sugars: 2.5g; Cholesterol: 21mg; Sodium: 2886mg

6.8 Mock Chili Relleno Soup

Serves: 4 Preparation Time: 6 minutes Cooking Time: 21 minutes

Ingredients:

- Unsalted Butter, 1 **tbsp.**
- Jalapeno Peppers, 4 pieces, seeded and chopped
- Onion, 1 small piece, peeled and chopped
- Thyme Leaves, 1 **tsp.**, dried and crushed
- Dried Cumin Seed, ½ **tsp.**, ground
- Salt
- Black Pepper, freshly ground
- Chicken Stock, 2 cups
- Cheddar Cheese, 6 oz., grated
- Heavy Cream, ¾ cup
- Cooked Bacon Slices, 4 pieces, chopped or crumbled

Procedure:

1. In a small skillet, melt the butter over a medium heat and sauté the jalapenos for 2 minutes until softened. Transfer the peppers to a plate with a slotted spoon. In the same pan, sauté the onions for 3 to 4 minutes until softened. Add the onions into the soup maker along with the thyme leaves, cumin, salt, pepper and stock. Secure the lid and program for smooth, timed at 21 minutes. Six minutes before the timer elapses, lift the lid and stir in the cooked jalapenos, bacon, cheese and cream. Let the soup finish cooking and transfer into bowls. Top with more bacon. Serve immediately.

Nutritional Facts: Cal: 2217; Carb: 24.2g; Protein: 82.7g; Fat: 199.3g; Fiber: 3.6g; Sugars: 7.5g; Cholesterol: 496mg; Sodium: 4678mg

6.9 Porky Bean Soup

Serves: 4 Preparation Time: 22 minutes Cooking Time: 28 minutes

Ingredients:

- Smoked Bacon, 6 oz,. chopped
- Onion, ½ cup, chopped
- Carrot, ½ cup, chopped
- Celery, ½ cup, chopped
- Garlic, 2 cloves, minced
- Navy Beans, 1 can, drained and rinsed
- Tomato Paste, 2 **tbsp.**s
- Sugar, 1 **tsp.**
- Thyme Leaves, fresh, 1 **tsp.**, chopped
- Salt
- Black Pepper, freshly ground
- Chicken Broth, 3 cups

Procedure:

1. In a medium skillet, cook the bacon over a medium flame for 8-10 minutes until fully cooked and fat has been rendered. Remove the bacon from the fat and allow to drain on a paper-towel lined plate. Crumble the bacon. Sauté the onions, carrots and celery in the rendered bacon fat for 3-4 minutes until softened. Add the garlic and cook for another minute. Transfer this into the soup maker along with the remainder of the ingredients. Secure the lid and program the soup maker for chunky, timed at 28 minutes. Once cooked, lift the lid and transfer into bowls. Garnish with the crumbled bacon and serve immediately.

Nutritional Facts: Cal: 1154; Carb: 86.9g; Protein: 81.3g; Fat: 94.2g; Fiber: 19.3g; Sugars: 16.2g; Cholesterol: 200mg; Sodium: 4474mg

6.10 Hearty Bacon Potato Chowder

Serves: 4 Preparation Time: 7 minutes Cooking Time: 28 minutes

Ingredients:

- Bacon Slices, 4 pieces
- Olive Oil, 1 **tsp.**
- Celery, 1 medium stalk, chopped
- Carrots, ½ cup, chopped
- Onion, ½ cup, chopped
- Potatoes, 2 cups, cubed
- Chicken Stock, low-sodium 3 cups
- Salt
- Black Pepper, freshly ground
- Cheddar Cheese, ¼ cup, grated

Procedure:

1. Cook the bacon in a skillet over medium heat for 8-10 minutes until fully cooked. Transfer the bacon to a paper towel lined plate and allow to drain. Crumble the bacon afterwards. In the rendered bacon fat, add the olive oil and sauté the onions, carrots and celery for 4-5 minutes until softened. Add this mirepoix into the soup maker along with the other ingredients except

the cheese. Secure the lid of the soup maker and program for chunky, with the timer set for 28 minutes. Once the soup has fully cooked, stir in the cheese and half the bacon. Transfer into bowls and garnish with the remaining bacon. Serve immediately.

Nutritional Facts: Cal: 1124; Carb: 43.3g; Protein: 62.6g; Fat: 78.2g; Fiber: 7.6g; Sugars: 11.5g; Cholesterol: 202mg; Sodium: 4992mg

6.11 Bacon and Pasta Soup

Serves: 4 Preparation Time: 15 minutes Cooking Time: 28 minutes

Ingredients:

- Olive Oil, 1 **tbsp.**
- Bacon, 2 oz., finely chopped as for lardons
- Onion, 1 medium piece, finely chopped
- Garlic, 2 cloves, minced
- Chicken Stock, 3 cups
- Italian Seasoning, 3 **tsp.**
- Cheese Tortellini, 4 oz.,
- Canned Tomatoes, 6 oz.
- Spinach, 4 oz., chopped
- Salt
- Black Pepper, freshly ground
- Parmesan Cheese, ¼ cup, grated

Procedure:

1. Heat the oil in a skillet over a medium flame and cook the bacon for 8-10 minutes until crisp. Sauté the onions in the rendered fat for 3-4 minutes. Add the garlic and cook for another minute. Add this mixture into the soup maker and add the remainder of the ingredients except for the Parmesan. Secure the lid and program for chunky at 28 minutes. Once the soup is cooked, lift the lid and transfer into bowls. Garnish with the Parmesan and serve immediately.

Nutritional Facts: Cal: 1306; Carb: 121.9g; Protein: 62.5g; Fat: 63.8g; Fiber: 3.4g; Sugars: 7g; Cholesterol: 134mg; Sodium: 5119mg

6.12 London Fog Soup

Serves: 1 Preparation Time: 5 minutes Cooking Time: 21 minutes

Ingredients:

- Canola Oil, 1 **tbsp.**
- Onion, 1 small, finely chopped
- Garlic, 1 clove, minced
- Cooked Ham, 8 oz., diced, reserve half of this
- Frozen Green Peas, thawed, 8 oz.
- Parsley, fresh, 2 **tbsp.**s, finely chopped
- Mint Leaves, 1 **tbsp.**
- Chicken Stock, 3 cups
- Salt
- Black Pepper, freshly ground

Procedure:

1. Heat the oil in a sauté pan over a medium flame and cook the onions for 3-4 minutes until softened. Add the garlic and cook for another minute. Transfer this into the soup maker and add half of the ham, all of the peas, the herbs, stock and seasonings. Secure the lid and program for smooth, set at 21 minutes. Once the soup is cooked, unlock the lid and stir in the rest of the ham. Transfer to bowls and serve immediately.

Nutritional Facts: Cal: 1450; Carb: 64.3g; Protein: 126.3g; Fat: 74.9g; Fiber: 21.9g; Sugars: 14g; Cholesterol: 388mg; Sodium: 11937mg

6.13 Bourbonnaise Cream Soup

Serves: 4 Preparation Time: 12 minutes Cooking Time: 28 minutes

Ingredients:

- Unsalted Butter, 1 **tbsp.**
- Onion, 1 small piece, minced
- Carrot, 1 small piece, diced
- Celery, 1 small stalk, chopped
- Potatoes, 2 cups, peeled and diced
- Garlic, 2 cloves, minced
- Cooked Ham, 1 cup, chopped
- Flour, 2 **tbsp.**s
- Chicken Stock, 2 cups
- Milk, 1 cup
- Black Pepper, freshly ground
- Cheddar Cheese, 4 **tbsp.**s

Procedure:

1. Heat the butter in a skillet over medium flame and cook the onions, carrots and celery for 3-4 minutes until softened. Add the ham and potatoes and cook for another 2 minutes. Add the garlic and cook for 1 minute. Stir in the flour and continue to cook for 2 minutes, toasting the flour and thickening the mixture. Transfer this into the soup maker and add the stock. Secure the lid and program for chunky at 28 minutes. Six minutes before the timer elapses, stir in the milk and pepper. Once the soup has fully cooked, transfer into bowls and garnish with the cheese before you serve.

Nutritional Facts: Cal: 740; Carb: 68g; Protein: 41.2g; Fat: 34.4g; Fiber: 8.9g; Sugars: 20g; Cholesterol: 142mg; Sodium: 3832mg

6.14 Ham and Corn Chowder

Serves: 4 Preparation Time: 7 minutes Cooking Time: 28 minutes

Ingredients:

- Olive Oil, 1 **tbsp.**
- Onion, 1 small piece, minced
- Potato, 1 cup, diced
- Red Bell Pepper, ½ cup, seeded and diced
- Thyme Leaves, dried, ½ **tsp.**
- Black Pepper, freshly ground
- Chicken Stock, 1 ½ cups

- Corn Kernels, 1 cup
- Ham, 1 cup, diced
- Flour, 2 **tbsp.**s
- Milk, 1 cup

Procedure:

1. Heat the oil in a skillet over medium heat and sauté the onions for 3-4 minutes until softened. Add the potatoes and bell peppers and season with the thyme and pepper. Cook for 2-3 minutes. Transfer this into the soup maker along with the corn, ham and stock. Secure the lid and program the soup maker for Chunky at 28 minutes. While the soup cooks, whisk the flour into the milk. Six minutes before the timer elapses, add the milk into the soup maker and stir. Once the cycle is completed, unlock the lid and serve immediately.

Nutritional Facts: Cal: 770; Carb: 84.8g; Protein: 40.4g; Fat: 33.5g; Fiber: 10.1g; Sugars: 22.5g; Cholesterol: 97mg; Sodium: 3520mg

6.15 Ham and Bean Pottage

Serves: 4 Preparation Time: 5 minutes Cooking Time: 28 minutes

Ingredients:

- Canned White Beans, 2 cups
- Ham, 1 ½ cups, diced
- Onion, 1 small, minced
- Garlic, 2 cloves, minced
- Water, 2 cups
- Italian Seasoning, 2 **tsp.**
- Salt
- Black Pepper, freshly ground
- Heavy Cream, ½ cup

Procedure:

1. Add all of the ingredients into the soup maker except for the cream. Secure the lid and program for chunky, set at 28 minutes. Six minutes before the timer elapses, lift the lid and stir in the cream. Secure lid to finish cooking. Once cooked, transfer into bowls and serve immediately.

Nutritional Facts: Cal: 1388; Carb: 130.8g; Protein: 77.4 g; Fat: 63.9g; Fiber: 31.3g; Sugars: 4.8g; Cholesterol: 278mg; Sodium: 5209mg

6.16 Southern Split Pea- Ham Soup

Serves: 4 Preparation Time: 5 minutes Cooking Time: 28 minutes

Ingredients:

- Unsalted Butter, 1 **tbsp.**
- Celery, 1 medium stalk, diced
- Onion, ½ cup, chopped
- Carrot, 1 small piece, peeled and diced
- Garlic, 2 cloves, thinly sliced
- Ham, 1 cup, diced
- Split Peas, canned, 2 cups, drained and rinsed
- Bay Leaf, 1 piece

- Chicken Stock, 3 cups
- Salt
- Black Pepper, freshly ground

Procedure:

1. Heat the butter in a skillet over a medium flame and sauté the onions, carrots and celery for 4-5 minutes or until softened. Transfer the mirepoix into the soup maker and add the rest of the ingredients. Secure the lid and program this for Chunky, timed at 28 minutes. Once the soup has fully cooked, transfer to bowls and serve immediately,

Nutritional Facts: Cal: 1768; Carb: 262.2g; Protein: 123.4g; Fat: 29.7g; Fiber: 106.4g; Sugars: 40.1g; Cholesterol: 107mg; Sodium: 4338mg

6.17 Curried Ham and Vegetable Soup

Serves: 4 Preparation Time: 10 minutes Cooking Time: 21 minutes

Ingredients:

- Cooking Spray, 1 second
- Cumin Seeds, 1 **tsp.**
- Onion, 1 large, peeled and diced
- Ham, 1 cup, diced
- Garlic, 2 cloves, minced
- Button Mushrooms, 2 cups, brushed, trimmed and quartered
- Frozen Peas, ½ cup, thawed
- Coriander Seed, ground, 1 **tbsp.**
- Ginger, ground, 1 **tbsp.**
- Chili, 1 piece, seeded and chopped
- Garam Masala, 1 **tsp.**
- Tomato Paste, 1 **tbsp.**
- Pork Stock Cube, 1 piece
- Water, 4 cups
- Salt
- Black Pepper, freshly ground

Procedure:

1. Spray a cooking pan with the spray and heat over a medium flame. Toast the cumin seeds for 3 minutes and set aside. Sauté the onions and garlic in the same pan until softened. Season the mixture with the spices and cook for another 2 minutes. Transfer this soffrito into the soup maker and add the remainder of the ingredients. Secure the lid of the soup maker and set for Chunky, programmed for 28 minutes. Once the soup is fully cooked, transfer into bowls and serve immediately.

Nutritional Facts: Cal: 424; Carb: 43.5g; Protein: 33.5g; Fat: 15.3g; Fiber: 12.4g; Sugars: 15g; Cholesterol: 77mg; Sodium: 2923mg

6.18 Bacon Vichysoisse

Serves: 4 Preparation Time: 10 minutes Cooking Time: 21 minutes

Ingredients:

- Cooking Spray, 1 second
- Onion, 1 whole, chopped

- Leek, 1 medium stalk, washed, and chopped
- Potatoes, 2 pieces, peeled and diced
- Skim Milk, ½ cup
- Water, 3 ½ cups
- Vegetable Stock, 2 cubes
- Bacon, 4 rashers fat trimmed
- Bacon Fat

Procedure:

1. Spray a pan with cooking spray and heat over a medium flame. Sauté the onions and bacon for 4-5 minutes until the onions have softened. Add the leeks and diced potatoes and stir to coat with the rendered fat from the bacon. Spray more cooking spray if needed. Reduce the heat to low and allow to cook for 5 minutes until the potatoes have softened.

2. Add all of the ingredients except the bacon into the soup maker and secure the lid. Program the soup maker for smooth and set the timer for 21 minutes. While the soup cooks, take the trimmed bacon fat and crisp it up in a pan. Crumble these. Once the soup is fully cooked, transfer into bowls and garnish with the bacon fat crumbles.

Nutritional Facts: Cal: 1863; Carb: 296.5g; Protein: 82.4g; Fat: 32.6g; Fiber: 15.3g; Sugars: 21.2g; Cholesterol: 86mg; Sodium: 1895mg

6.19 Irish Bacon Soup

Serves: 4 Preparation Time: 10 minutes Cooking Time: 21 minutes

Ingredients:

- Cooking Spray, 1 second
- Potatoes, 3 cups, diced
- Savoy Cabbage, ¼ of a head (you may use a smaller head of cabbage)
- Onion, 1 large piece, peeled and diced
- Carrot, 1 large, peeled and diced
- Celery, 1 large stalk, diced
- Garlic, 1 clove, peeled and minced
- Rosemary Leaves, dried, 1 **tsp.**
- Salt
- Black Pepper, freshly ground
- Water, 3 cups
- Chicken Stock Cubes, 2 pieces
- Bacon, 8 rashers, fat trimmed

Procedure:

1. Spray a pan with the cooking spray and heat over a medium flame. Cook the onions, carrots and celery for 4-5 minutes until softened. Add the potatoes, cabbage and rosemary leaves and spray with more cooking spray. Cover with a lid and lower the heat. Cook for 10 minutes until potatoes have softened.

2. Add all of these into the soup maker and program it for smooth, set at 21 minutes. While the soup cooks, cook the bacon until crisp and crumble it. Once the soup is fully cooked, transfer into bowls and garnish with the crumbled bacon.

Nutritional Facts: Cal: 1124; Carb: 68.9g; Protein: 65.8g; Fat: 64.7g; Fiber: 14.2g; Sugars: 15g; Cholesterol: 168mg; Sodium: 6133mg

6.20 Sausage and Gnocchi Soup

Serves: 2 Preparation Time: 10 minutes Cooking Time: 21 minutes

Ingredients:

- Red Bell Pepper, 1 medium piece, seeded and chopped
- Celery, 2 small stalks, chopped
- Onion 1 small piece, peeled and chopped
- Garlic, 2 cloves, crushed
- Fennel Seed, ground, 1 **tsp.**
- Beef Stock, 2 ¾ cups
- Tomato Puree, 2 cups
- Olive Oil, 2 **tbsp.**s
- Potato Gnocchi, 1 500g pack
- Pork Sausages, 2 links
- Parmesan Cheese, Lemon Zest, Pepper, Rosemary Leaves for garnish

Procedure:

1. Add the bell peppers, celery, onions, garlic, fennel seed and beef stock into the soup maker. Season with salt. Secure the lid and program it for Chunky. Time this for 21 minutes.
2. Heat the oil in a pan over a medium flame and fry the gnocchi until lightly browned and tender. Transfer this to a bowl. Remove the sausage from its casings and roll the meat into balls. Fry these in a pan for 3 minutes until browned.
3. Transfer the soup into bowls and add the gnocchi and sausage. Garnish with shaved parmesan, pepper, lemon zest and some rosemary leaves. Serve immediately.

Nutritional Facts: Cal: 1659; Carb: 269g; Protein: 55.2g; Fat: 43.8g; Fiber: 28.6g; Sugars: 37.6g; Cholesterol: 110mg; Sodium: 5058mg

6.21 Chorizo and Bean Soup

Serves: 4 Preparation Time: 10 minutes Cooking Time: 21 minutes

Ingredients:

- Carrot, 1 small piece, diced
- Swede, 1 piece, cubed
- Onion, 1 small piece, peeled and diced
- Celery, 1 small stalk, diced
- Frozen Peas, 1 cup, thawed
- Salt
- Canned Tomatoes, 2 cans, liquid reserved, diced
- Chicken Stock, 2 cups
- Tomato Paste, 2 **tbsp.**s
- Chorizo, 2 links
- Canned Mixed Beans, 1 can, drained and rinsed
- Feta Cheese
- Oregano Leaves

Procedure:

1. Add the carrot, swede, onion, celery, canned tomatoes, chicken stock and tomato paste into the soup maker and season with the salt. Secure the lid and program for Chunky, timed at 21 minutes.
2. While the soup cooks, heat a skillet over a medium flame and cook the chorizo. Cook until browned. Add the peas and beans into the soup maker. Secure the lid and cook for 5 more minutes in the soup maker to heat the beans and peas. Transfer into bowls and top with the cooked chorizo. Serve immediately.

Nutritional Facts: Cal: 1385; Carb: 113g; Protein: 79.1g; Fat: 69.5g; Fiber: 27.3g; Sugars: 23.3g; Cholesterol: 244mg; Sodium: 4976mg

6.22 Prosciutto, Peas and Bean Soup

Serves: 4 Preparation Time: 10 minutes Cooking Time: 21 minutes

Ingredients:

- Frozen Peas, 500 grams, thawed
- Frozen Broad Beans, 200 grams, thawed and shelled
- Potato, 2 medium pieces, diced
- Onion, 1 piece, peeled and chopped
- Garlic, 2 cloves, crushed
- Vegetable Stock, 3 1/3 cups
- Cream, 1/3 cup
- Prosciutto, 3 slices
- Chives
- Sour Cream

Procedure:

1. Add the peas, beans, potatoes, onions, garlic and stock into the soup maker and secure the lid. Program for Smooth and set the time for 21 minutes. Once the soup is cooked, season with salt and stir in the cream. Blend for 15 minutes in the soup maker and transfer into bowls.
2. While the soup cooks, cook the prosciutto in a non-stick skillet over a medium flame until crisp. Crumble or chop and use to garnish the soup along with the chives and sour cream. Serve the soup immediately.

Nutritional Facts: Cal: 1411; Carb: 190.1g; Protein: 72.4g; Fat: 49.7g; Fiber: 52.2g; Sugars: 39.3g; Cholesterol: 164mg; Sodium: 4112mg

6.23 Quick and Peasy Pancetta Soup

Serves: 4 Preparation Time: 5 minutes Cooking Time: 25 minutes

Ingredients:

- Olive Oil, 1 **tbsp.**
- Pancetta, 200 grams, chopped
- Onion, 1 small piece, finely chopped
- Leek, 1 piece, rinsed, trimmed and finely chopped
- Garlic, 2 cloves, crushed
- Frozen Peas, ¾ cup, thawed
- Chicken Stock, 4 cups
- Thyme Leaves, dried, 1 **tsp.**

Procedure:

1. Set the soup maker for 25 minutes on simmer. Add the oil and allow to heat for 30 seconds before the pancetta is added. Cook the pancetta for 1-2 minutes and add the leeks and onions. Cook for 4-5 minutes until softened.

2. Turn the soup maker to its highest setting and add the garlic, peas, stock, and thyme. Add salt and pepper, then bring to a boil. Reduce the heat to a simmer and finish cooking the soup. Remove the soup from the heat and puree it in a soup maker until smooth. Immediately transfer to bowls and serve.

Nutritional Facts: Cal: 1407; Carb: 40.1g; Protein: 83.8g; Fat: 101g; Fiber: 7.2g; Sugars: 12.3g; Cholesterol: 222mg; Sodium: 7775mg

6.24 Bacon and Lentil Soup

Serves: 4 Preparation Time: 5 minutes Cooking Time: 30 minutes

Ingredients:

- Olive Oil, 1 **tbsp.**
- Smoked Bacon, 200 grams, finely chopped
- Onion, 1 piece, finely chopped
- Carrots, 2 pieces, peeled and chopped
- Chicken Stock, 3 ½ cups
- Red Lentils, 150 grams, washed
- Parsley Leaves, fresh, finely chopped

Procedure:

1. Preset the soup maker for simmer on 30 minutes. Add the olive oil and cook the bacon for 2 minutes until crisp. Add the onions and carrots and cook for 7 minutes until softened. Pour the stock and add the lentils. Season with salt and pepper and adjust the settings of the soup maker on high until the soup boils. Lower the heat to simmer and allow to finish cooking, adding 5-10 minutes if the lentils are not softened. Puree the soup until smooth and transfer into bowls and serve immediately.

Nutritional Facts: Cal: 1821; Carb: 110.7g; Protein: 115.3g; Fat: 100.9g; Fiber: 48.6g; Sugars: 14.4g; Cholesterol: 219mg; Sodium: 7379mg

6.25 Yuletide Leftover Soup (25)

Serves: 4 Preparation Time: 5 minutes Cooking Time: 30 minutes

Ingredients:

- Pigs in Blankets, 2 pieces
- Mashed Potatoes, 1 **tbsp.**
- Mashed Carrot, 3 **tbsp.**s
- Cauliflower Cheese, 2 **tbsp.**s
- Turkey Breast, 200 grams, sliced thinly
- Roasted Potatoes, 4 pieces, cubed
- Gravy, 1 cup
- Turkey Stuffing, 3 **tbsp.**s
- Vegetable Stock 3 cups
- Thyme Leaves, dried, 1 **tbsp.**
- Parsley Leaves, dried, 1 **tbsp.**

- Salt
- Black Pepper, freshly ground
- Water, 1 cup

Procedure:

1. Add all of the ingredients into the soup maker except for the herbs and seasonings. Secure the lid of soup maker and program for smooth set at 28 minutes. Use the blender function and puree the soup to your desired consistency. Thin the soup with more stock if needed. Season the soup with the herbs and seasonings. Transfer into bowls and serve immediately.

Nutritional Facts: Cal: 167; Carb: 7g; Protein: 13g; Fat: 10g; Fiber: 1g; Sugars: 2g; Cholesterol: 38mg; Sodium: 586mg

7 SEAFOOD

7.1 Lox and Schmear Soup

Serves: 4 Preparation Time: 5 minutes Cooking Time: 21 minutes

Ingredients:

- Unsalted Butter, 2 **tbsp.**s
- Celery, 1 stalk, chopped
- Onion, ½ cup, chopped
- Salt, ½ **tsp.**
- Garlic, 1 clove, minced
- Chicken Stock, 1 ½ cups
- Tomato Paste, 1 **tbsp.**
- Cream Cheese, 4 oz., softened
- Smoked Salmon, 8 oz., chopped

Procedure:

1. Heat the butter in a medium pan over a medium flame and sauté the celery and onions for 4-5 minutes. Season with salt. Add the garlic and cook for another minute. Transfer this mirepoix into the soup maker along with the stock and tomato paste. Secure the lid of the soup maker and set it for smooth, programmed for 21 minutes. Six minutes before the timer elapses, lift the lid and stir in the cream cheese and salmon. Once the soup has fully cooked, lift the lid and transfer into bowls and serve immediately.

Nutritional Facts: Cal: 1469; Carb: 17.5g; Protein: 136.3g; Fat: 93g; Fiber: 3.5g; Sugars: 7.5g; Cholesterol: 342mg; Sodium: 15309mg

7.2 Creamy Salmon Chowder

Serves: 4 Preparation Time: 5 minutes Cooking Time: 28 minutes

Ingredients:

- Chicken Stock, 1 cup
- Flour, 1 **tbsp.**
- Milk, 2 cups
- Salmon, 1 (16 oz.) can, deboned
- Black Pepper, freshly ground
- Salt
- Parsley Leaves, fresh, 2 **tbsp.**s

Procedure:

1. Mix the flour and stock in a bowl until the flour has dissolved. Add this into the soup maker along with the remainder of the ingredients except the parsley. Secure the lid and program for chunky, timed at 28 minutes. Once the soup is cooked, lift the lid and transfer into bowls. Garnish with parsley and serve immediately.

Nutritional Facts: Cal: 2570; Carb: 36.9g; Protein: 335.8g; Fat: 110.2g; Fiber: 0.7g; Sugars: 22.8g; Cholesterol: 638mg; Sodium: 6248mg

7.3 Summer Salmon Chowder

Serves: 4 Preparation Time: 11 minutes Cooking Time: 28 minutes

Ingredients:

- Unsalted Butter, 1 **tbsp.**
- Onion, ¼ cup, chopped
- Celery, ¼ cup, chopped
- Garlic Powder, 1 **tsp.**
- Potatoes, 1 cup, diced
- Carrot, 1 piece, peeled and chopped
- Chicken Stock, 2 cups
- Salt
- Black Pepper, freshly ground
- Canned Salmon, 8 oz,
- Creamed Corn, 6 oz.,
- Cheddar Cheese, ¼ cup, grated
- Evaporated Milk, ¼ cup

Procedure:

1. Heat the butter in a pan over a medium flame and sauté the onions and celery for 4-5 minutes. Season with the garlic powder. Add the potatoes, carrots and half the stock and allow to cook for 3-4 minutes. Transfer this into the soup maker and add the remainder of the broth and seasonings. Secure the lid and program for chunky, timed at 28 minutes. Eight minutes before the timer elapses, lift the lid and add the remainder of the ingredients. Once the soup has finished cooking, lift the lid, transfer into bowls and serve immediately.

Nutritional Facts: Cal: 1630; Carb: 116.8g; Protein: 153.5g; Fat: 68.6g; Fiber: 10.7g; Sugars: 26.9g; Cholesterol: 369mg; Sodium: 3635mg

7.4 Summer Salmon Broth

Serves: 4 Preparation Time: 5 minutes Cooking Time: 28 minutes

Ingredients:

- Olive Oil, 1 **tbsp.**
- Onion, 1 whole piece, chopped
- Garlic, 1 clove, minced
- Chicken Broth, 3 cups
- Boneless Salmon Fillet, ¾ pound, cubed
- Soy Sauce, low-sodium, 1 **tbsp.**
- Fresh Parsley, 2 **tbsp.**s, chopped
- Black Pepper, freshly ground
- Lime Juice, 1 **tbsp.**

Procedure:

1. Heat the oil in a medium saucepan over a medium flame and sauté the onions for 5 minutes until softened. Add the garlic and cook for another minute. Transfer this into a soup maker and add the remainder of the ingredients. Secure the lid and program the soup maker for chunky at 28 minutes. Once the soup is fully cooked, transfer into bowls and serve immediately.

Nutritional Facts: Cal: 546; Carb: 20.3g; Protein: 52.3g; Fat: 29.3g; Fiber: 3.6g; Sugars: 9.8g; Cholesterol: 78mg; Sodium: 3318mg

7.5 Eastern Salmon Soup

Serves: 4 Preparation Time: 5 minutes Cooking Time: 28 minutes

Ingredients:

- Cooked Rice, 1 cup
- Skinless Salmon Fillet, ¾ lb, cubed
- Soy Sauce, low-sodium, 2 **tbsp.**s
- Sesame Oil, 1 **tbsp.**
- Cilantro, fresh, 2 **tbsp.**s chopped
- Ginger, 1 **tbsp.**, minced
- Salt
- Chicken Broth, 3 cups
- Scallions, 2 stalks, chopped

Procedure:

1. Add all of the ingredients into the soup maker except for the scallions, and secure the lid. Program for chunky, set at 28 minutes. Once the soup has been fully cooked, transfer into bowls and garnish with the scallions. Serve immediately.

Nutritional Facts: Cal: 2480; Carb: 54.8g; Protein: 242.3g; Fat: 138.2g; Fiber: 2.1g; Sugars: 4.9g; Cholesterol: 650mg; Sodium: 4877mg

7.6 Salmon and Greened Quinoa Soup

Serves: 4 Preparation Time: 10 minutes Cooking Time: 28 minutes

Ingredients:

- Olive Oil, 1 **tbsp.**
- Button Mushrooms, ½ cup, sliced
- Onions, ¼ cup, chopped
- Celery, ¼ cup, chopped
- Garlic, 1 clove, chopped
- Ginger, 1 **tsp.**, grated
- Quinoa, ¾ cup, cooked
- Salmon Fillets, 6 oz., cubed
- Baby Spinach, 2 cups
- Vegetable Stock, 2 cups
- Salt
- Coconut Milk, ½ cup

Procedure:

1. Heat the oil in a medium saucepan over a medium flame and sauté the mushrooms, onions and celery for 5-6 minutes. Add the garlic and ginger and cook for another minute. Transfer this into the soup maker and add the remainder of the ingredients except for the coconut milk. Secure the lid and set for chunky, timed at 28 minutes. Six minutes before the timer elapses, add the coconut milk and allow to finish cooking. Transfer into bowls and serve immediately.

Nutritional Facts: Cal: 1944; Carb: 189.6g; Protein: 141.9g; Fat: 86g; Fiber: 52.9g; Sugars: 10.4g; Cholesterol: 225mg; Sodium: 3202mg

7.7 Salmon, Cabbage and Mushroom Soup

Serves: 4 Preparation Time: 10 minutes Cooking Time: 28 minutes

Ingredients:

- Olive Oil, 1 **tbsp.**
- Onion, 1 small piece, chopped
- Cabbage, 2 cups, shredded
- Button Mushrooms, 1 cup, brushed, trimmed and sliced
- Chicken Stock, 3 cups
- Salmon Fillets, deboned, 2 4 oz., pieces, cubed
- Cilantro Leaves, 2 **tbsp.**s, minced
- Lemon Juice, 1 **tbsp.**
- Salt
- Black Pepper, freshly ground

Procedure:

1. Heat the olive oil in a skillet over a medium flame and sauté the onions for 4-5 minutes until softened. Add the cabbage and mushrooms and cook for an additional 5 minutes. Transfer this into the Soup Maker and add the remainder of the ingredients. Secure the lid and program for Chunky, timed at 28 minutes. Once the soup has fully cooked, transfer into bowls and serve immediately.

Nutritional Facts: Cal: 1129; Carb: 19.8g; Protein: 138.8g; Fat: 58.1g; Fiber: 5.8g; Sugars: 11.5g; Cholesterol: 300mg; Sodium: 2778mg

7.8 Bacalhau con Tomate Soup

Serves: 4 Preparation Time: 5 minutes Cooking Time: 28 minutes

Ingredients:

- Cod Fillets, 8 oz., cut into ½ inch cubes
- Canned Tomatoes, diced, 1 (14.5 oz.) can, reserve liquid
- Onion, ½ cup, chopped
- Celery, ½ cup, chopped
- Garlic, 1 clove, minced
- Thyme Leaves, dried, ½ **tsp.**
- Clam Juice, 2 cups
- Chicken Stock, ½ cup
- Salt
- Black Pepper, freshly ground

Procedure:

1. Add all of the ingredients into the soup maker. Secure the lid and program it for Chunky, timed at 28 minutes. Once the soup has been fully cooked, lift the lid carefully and transfer into bowls. Serve immediately.

Nutritional Facts: Cal: 379; Carb: 44.5g; Protein: 44.9g; Fat: 3.3g; Fiber: 5.7g; Sugars: 12.5g; Cholesterol: 110mg; Sodium: 1728mg

7.9 New England Style Cod Soup

Serves: 4 Preparation Time: 5 minutes Cooking Time: 28 minutes

Ingredients:

- Olive Oil, 1 **tbsp.**
- Celery, 1 medium stalk, chopped
- Onion, ½ cup, chopped
- Garlic, 2 cloves, minced
- Tomato Paste, 2 **tbsp.**s
- Thyme Leaves, dried, 2 **tsp.**
- Potatoes, 2 cups, peeled and chopped
- Canned Tomatoes, diced, 1 (14.5oz) can, reserve liquid
- Chicken Stock, 2 cups
- Cod, 8 oz., cut into even chunks
- Black Pepper, freshly ground
- Parsley leaves, fresh, 2 **tbsp.**s, chopped

Procedure:

1. Add all of the ingredients into the soup maker except for the parsley. Secure the lid and program it for Chunky, timed at 28 minutes. Once the soup has been fully cooked, lift the lid carefully and transfer into bowls. Garnish with the parsley and serve immediately.

Nutritional Facts: Cal: 1058; Carb: 47.9g; Protein: 163.4g; Fat: 21.9g; Fiber: 9.7g; Sugars: 9.2g; Cholesterol: 374mg; Sodium: 2370mg

7.10 Tilapia Soup

Serves: 4 Preparation Time: 5 minutes Cooking Time: 28 minutes

Ingredients:

- Chicken Stock, 2 cups
- Spinach, fresh, 2 cups, chopped
- Button Mushrooms, ½ cup, brushed and sliced
- Tilapia Fillets, 2 (4 oz.,) pieces, cut into even cubes
- Fish Sauce, 1 **tsp.**
- Salt
- Black Pepper, freshly ground
- Scallions, 2 **tbsp.**s, chopped

Procedure:

1. Add all of the ingredients into the soup maker except for the scallions. Secure the lid and program it for Chunky, timed at 28 minutes. Once the soup has been fully cooked, lift the lid carefully and transfer into bowls. Garnish with the scallions and serve immediately.

Nutritional Facts: Cal: 788; Carb: 5.5g; Protein: 172.5g; Fat: 9.6g; Fiber: 1.8g; Sugars: 2.6g; Cholesterol: 440mg; Sodium: 2748mg

7.11 Halibut Soup

Serves: 4 Preparation Time: 5 minutes Cooking Time: 28 minutes

Ingredients:

- Halibut Fillets, 10 oz., chopped

- Parsley Leaves, fresh, ¼ cup, chopped
- Garlic, 2 cloves, minced
- Tomatoes, 2, seeded and chopped
- Anchovies, oil-packed, 2 fillets, chopped
- Red Pepper Flakes, 2 **tsp.**, crushed
- Salt
- Black Pepper, freshly ground
- Chicken Stock, 3 cups

Procedure:

1. Add all of the ingredients into the soup maker. Secure the lid and program it for Chunky, timed at 28 minutes. Once the soup has been fully cooked, lift the lid carefully and transfer into bowls. Serve immediately.

Nutritional Facts: Cal: 188; Carb: 16g; Protein: 18.4g; Fat: 6.8g; Fiber: 3.4g; Sugars: 6.1g; Cholesterol: 37mg; Sodium: 3936mg

7.12 Snapper Soup Indienne

Serves: 4 Preparation Time: 5 minutes Cooking Time: 28 minutes

Ingredients:

- Olive Oil, 1 tbsp.
- Salt
- Celery, 1 small stalk, chopped
- Paprika, ½ tsp.
- Onion, 1 small piece, peeled and chopped
- Turmeric, ½ tsp., ground
- Bell Pepper, 1 small piece, seeded and chopped
- Dried Cumin Seed, ½ tsp., ground
- Garlic, 2 cloves, peeled and minced
- Snapper Fillets, 10 oz., cut into small pieces
- Dried Coriander Seed, ½ tsp., ground
- Black Pepper, freshly ground
- Whole Tomatoes, canned, 1 (14oz.) can, chopped with liquid reserved
- White Wine, ½ cup
- Chicken Stock, 2 cups
- Parsley Leaves, fresh, 2 **tbsp.**s, chopped
- Lemon Juice, 1 **tbsp.**

Procedure:

1. Heat the olive oil in a large skillet over a medium flame. Sauté the onions, celery, bell peppers and garlic for 4-5 minutes until softened and fragrant. Transfer this into the soup maker and add the other ingredients except for the parsley and lemon juice. Secure the lid and program for Chunky, set at 28 minutes. Once the soup is cooked, carefully lift the lid and stir in the parsley and lemon juice. Transfer into bowls and serve immediately.

Nutritional Facts: Cal: 351; Carb: 27.7g; Protein: 8.9g; Fat: 16.7g; Fiber: 6.8g; Sugars: 8.3g; Cholesterol: 5mg; Sodium: 1870mg

7.13 Summer Squash Shrimp Soup

Serves: 4 Preparation Time: 5 minutes Cooking Time: 28 minutes

Ingredients:

- Large Shrimp, 10 oz., shelled and deveined
- Zucchini, 8 oz., chopped
- Cilantro, fresh, 2 tbsp.s, chopped
- Scallions, 2 stalks, sliced
- Red Chili, 1 piece, seeded and chopped
- Ginger, 1 tsp., grated
- Kaffir Lime Leaves, 2 pieces
- Fish Sauce, 2 tbsp.s
- Chicken Stock, 3 cups
- Lime Juice, 1 tbsp.

Procedure:

1. Add all of the ingredients into the soup maker except for the lime juice. Secure the lid and program it for Chunky, timed at 28 minutes. Once the soup has been fully cooked, lift the lid carefully, stir in the lime juice and transfer into bowls. Serve immediately.

Nutritional Facts: Cal: 1063; Carb: 50.3g; Protein: 220.6g; Fat: 2.9g; Fiber: 6.9g; Sugars: 12.7g; Cholesterol: 1600mg; Sodium: 6576mg

7.14 Shrimp and Mushroom Bisque

Serves: 4 Preparation Time: 10 minutes Cooking Time: 28 minutes

Ingredients:

- Butter, 1 **tbsp.**
- Onion, ½ cup, chopped
- Oyster Mushrooms, 1 cup
- Garlic, 2 cloves, minced
- Chicken Stock, 2 cups
- Shrimp, 10 oz., shelled and deveined
- Cajun Seasoning, ½ **tsp.**
- Salt
- Black Pepper, freshly ground
- Heavy Cream, 1 cup
- Parsley Leaves, fresh, 2 **tbsp.**s

Procedure:

1. In a skillet heated over medium heat, sauté the onions, mushrooms, and garlic for 4-5 minutes, or until tender. Stir regularly. Transfer this to a soup maker and add the remaining ingredients, with the exception of the cream and parsley. Secure the lid and set the timer for 28 minutes for Chunky. Before the timer expires, carefully remove the lid and whisk in the heavy cream and parsley. Allow to cook until done, then transfer to bowls. Serve without delay.

Nutritional Facts: Cal: 1924; Carb: 45.1g; Protein: 221.6g; Fat: 101.3g; Fiber: 4.7g; Sugars: 6.5g; Cholesterol: 1957mg; Sodium: 3290mg

7.15 Snow Pea and Shrimp Broth

Serves: 8 Preparation Time: 5 minutes Cooking Time: 28 minutes

Ingredients:

- Shrimps, 10 oz., shelled and deveined
- Bamboo Shoots, canned, 4 oz., drained and sliced
- Snow Peas, 1 cup, trimmed
- Scallions, 2 stalks, thinly sliced
- Ginger, 1 inch piece, thinly sliced
- Chicken Stock, 3 cups
- Fish Sauce, 1 **tsp.**
- Soy Sauce, low-sodium, 2 **tbsp.**s
- White Pepper, ground
- Toasted Sesame Oil, 1 **tbsp.**

Procedure:

1. Add all of the ingredients into the soup maker except for the Sesame Oil. Secure the lid and program the soup maker for Chunky set at 28 minutes. Once the soup is cooked, lift the lid and stir in the sesame oil. Transfer into bowls and serve immediately.

Nutritional Facts: Cal: 937; Carb: 36.6g; Protein: 169.4g; Fat: 16.1g; Fiber: 5.2g; Sugars: 11.6g; Cholesterol: 1214mg; Sodium: 5826mg

7.16 Quick Lobster Bisque

Serves: 4 Preparation Time: 5 minutes Cooking Time: 21 minutes

Ingredients:

- Olive Oil, 1 **tbsp.**
- Carrot, 1 medium piece, peeled and diced
- Celery, 1 medium stalk, chopped
- Onion, 1 small piece, peeled and chopped
- Garlic, 2 cloves, peeled and minced
- Chicken Stock, 2 cups
- White Wine, ½ cup
- Tomato Paste, 2 **tbsp.**s
- Old Bay Seasoning, 1 **tsp.**
- Heavy Cream, ½ cup
- Lobster Meat from the Claw, 10 oz.,
- Butter, 1 **tbsp.**
- Garlic, 2 cloves, minced
- Lemon Juice, 1 **tbsp.**

Procedure:

1. Add all of the ingredients except for the heavy cream, lobster, butter, garlic and lemon juice into the soup maker and program for smooth set at 21 minutes. Six minutes before the timer elapses, stir in the heavy cream and allow to finish cooking.
2. While the soup cooks, heat the butter in a skillet over medium flame and sauté the lobster meat with the garlic for 4-5 minutes. Finish with the lemon juice. Once the soup is cooked, transfer into bowls and top with the cooked lobster meat. Stir and serve immediately.

Nutritional Facts: Cal: 1280; Carb: 40.3g; Protein: 99.3g; Fat: 71.2g; Fiber: 5.8g; Sugars: 14.6g; Cholesterol: 493mg; Sodium: 5534mg

7.17 Quickfire Crab Bisque

Serves: 4 Preparation Time: 10 minutes Cooking Time: 21 minutes

Ingredients:

- Unsalted Butter, 1 **tbsp.**
- Onion, 1 small, peeled and diced
- Garlic, 2 cloves, peeled and minced
- Flour, 2 **tbsp.**s
- Chicken Stock, 2 ½ cups
- Baby Potatoes, 10 oz., cubed
- Old Bay Seasoning, 1 **tbsp.**
- Salt
- Black Pepper, freshly ground
- Crab Meat, 8 oz., shelled
- Half and Half, ½ cup
- Balsamic Vinegar, 2 **tsp.**
- Parsley Leaves, fresh, 2 **tbsp.**s, chopped

Procedure:

1. Heat the butter in a skillet over a medium flame and sauté the onion for 4-6 minutes until softened. Add the garlic and cook for a minute until aromatic. Stir in the flour to make a roux with the onion and garlic and cook for a minute, stirring frequently. Add the garlic and onion roux into the soup maker and add the remainder of the ingredients except for the crab meat, half and half, vinegar and parsley.
2. Secure the lid and program for smooth, set for 21 minutes. Eight minutes before the timer elapses, stir in the crab meat, half and half and vinegar. Allow to finish cooking. Once the soup is cooked, lift the lid and stir in the parsley. Transfer into bowls and serve immediately.

Nutritional Facts: Cal: 1807; Carb: 332.8g; Protein: 61.6g; Fat: 38.7g; Fiber: 40g; Sugars: 20.1g; Cholesterol: 145mg; Sodium: 3491mg

7.18 New England Clam Chowder

Serves: 4 Preparation Time: 10 minutes Cooking Time: 21 minutes

Ingredients:

- Olive Oil, 1 **tbsp.**
- Onion, 1 small piece, peeled and chopped
- Celery, 1 small stalk, chopped
- Garlic, 1 clove, peeled and minced
- Potatoes, 2 small pieces, peeled and chopped
- Clam Juice, 1 8oz. bottle
- Water, 1 cup
- Thyme Leaves, ½ **tsp.**, crushed
- White Pepper, ¼ **tsp.**
- Half and Half, ¾ cup

- Canned Clams, 10 oz., chopped
- Parsley Leaves, 2 **tbsp.**s, chopped

Procedure:

1. Heat the olive oil in a skillet over medium heat and sauté the onions and celery for 4-5 minutes until softened. Add the garlic and cook for another minute. Transfer this into the soup maker and add the remainder of the ingredients except for the half and half, clam meat and parsley.
2. Secure the lid and program for Smooth, set at 21 minutes. Eight minutes before the timer elapses, add the half and half and clam meat and stir. Allow to finish cooking. Transfer into bowls and garnish with the parsley. Serve immediately.

Nutritional Facts: Cal: 797; Carb: 100.9g; Protein: 21.9g; Fat: 35.9g; Fiber: 11.6g; Sugars: 15.5g; Cholesterol: 87mg; Sodium: 1698mg

7.19 Seafood Mix Soup

Serves: 4 Preparation Time: 7 minutes Cooking Time: 28 minutes

Ingredients:

- Butter, 1 **tbsp.**
- Celery, ½ cup, chopped
- Garlic, 2 cloves, minced
- Salmon Fillets, deboned, 4 oz., cut into cubes
- Shrimp, 6 oz., shelled and deveined
- Spinach, 2 cups, chopped
- Clam Juice, 1 cup
- Chicken Stock, 2 cups
- Lemon Juice, 1 **tbsp.**
- Thyme Leaves, dried, 2 **tsp.**
- Lemon Zest, 1 **tsp.**
- Salt
- Black Pepper, freshly ground

Procedure:

1. Heat the butter in a skillet over a medium flame and sauté the celery and garlic for 5-7 minutes until softened. Transfer to the soup maker and add the remainder of the ingredients and secure the lid. Program for Chunky set at 28 minutes. Once the soup is cooked, carefully lift the lid and transfer into bowls. Serve immediately.

Nutritional Facts: Cal: 1157; Carb: 24.8g; Protein: 179.6g; Fat: 40.5g; Fiber: 4.1g; Sugars: 7.4g; Cholesterol: 1170mg; Sodium: 3475mg

7.20 Caribbean Seafood Soup

Serves: 4 Preparation Time: 5 minutes Cooking Time: 28 minutes

Ingredients:

- Chicken Stock, 2 cups
- Onion, ½ cup, chopped
- Button Mushrooms, 1 cup, brushed and sliced
- Kale, 1 cup, midribs removed, and leaves chopped
- Tilapia Fillets, 2 4 oz. fillets, cubed
- Shrimp, 4 oz., shelled and deveined

- Fish Sauce, 1 **tsp.**
- Salt
- Black Pepper, freshly ground
- Coconut Cream, 1 cup

Procedure:

1. Add all of the ingredients into the soup maker except for the coconut cream. Secure the lid and program for Chunky, set at 28 minutes. Eight minutes before the timer elapses, lift the lid carefully and stir in the coconut cream. Allow to finish cooking. Transfer into bowls and serve immediately.

Nutritional Facts: Cal: 2224; Carb: 176.1g; Protein: 250.5g; Fat: 61.8g; Fiber: 4g; Sugars: 158.8g; Cholesterol: 1100mg; Sodium: 3600mg

7.21 Seafood Noodle Soup

Serves: 4 Preparation Time: 20 minutes Cooking Time: 21 minutes

Ingredients:

- Cooking Spray, 1 second spray
- Fish Fillets, 2 pieces, thawed
- Onion, 1 medium piece, peeled and diced
- Ginger, 3 **tsp.**, grated
- Garlic, 3 cloves, peeled and minced
- Chili Pepper, 1 piece, seeded and chopped
- Cauliflower, 1 small head, broken into florets
- Egg Noodles, 90 grams
- Sweet Corn Kernels, ¼ cup
- Fish Sauce, 2 **tbsp.**s
- Water, 1 liter
- Salt
- Black Pepper, freshly ground
- Lemon Juice, from half a lemon
- Soy Sauce, 1 ¼ **tbsp.**s
- Parsley Leaves, 1 **tbsp.**

Procedure:

1. Spray a grill pan with cooking spray and heat over a medium flame. Grill the fish fillets on a grill pan and turn to cook the other side. Flake the cooked fish and set aside.
2. Spray cooking spray on a skillet and heat over a medium flame. Sauté the onions for 5-10 minutes until softened. Add the ginger, garlic and chilies and cook for another 3 minutes.
3. Transfer to the soup maker and add the remainder of the ingredients except ¼ **tsp.** soy sauce, parsley and lemon juice. Stir in the flaked and cooked fish and secure the lid. Set the soup maker for Chunky and time for 28 minutes. Once cooked, lift the lid and stir in the soy sauce, lemon juice and parsley. Transfer into bowls and serve immediately.

Nutritional Facts: Cal: 744; Carb: 96.2g; Protein: 42.6g; Fat: 25.2g; Fiber: 12.9g; Sugars: 19.6g; Cholesterol: 85mg; Sodium: 5255mg

7.22 Seafood Chowder

Serves: 4 Preparation Time: 20 minutes Cooking Time: 21 minutes

Ingredients:

- Cooking Spray, 1 second
- Onion, 1 large piece, chopped
- Celery, 1 large stalk, diced
- Garlic, 1 clove, minced
- Mixed Seafood, 325 grams
- Potato, 1 large piece, peeled and cubed
- Skim Milk, ½ cup
- Bay Leaf, 1 piece
- Parsley Leaves, dried, 1 **tsp.**
- Lemon Juice, 1 **tsp.**
- Cayenne Pepper, 1/8 **tsp.**
- Fish Stock Cubes, 2 pieces
- Water, 3 cups
- Salt
- Black Pepper, freshly ground

Procedure:

1. Spray a skillet with the cooking spray and heat over a medium flame. Sauté the onions, celery, garlic and potatoes until the onions and potatoes have softened. Add the seafood and cook for 3 minutes. Transfer this into the soup maker and add the remainder of the ingredients. Program for Chunky set at 21 minutes. Once the soup is cooked, use the blender function to blend the soup for a smoother texture. Transfer into bowls and serve immediately.

Nutritional Facts: Cal: 568; Carb: 62.8g; Protein: 59.7g; Fat: 3.7g; Fiber: 8.7g; Sugars: 16.1g; Cholesterol: 350mg; Sodium: 1449mg

7.23 Fish Curry

Serves: 4 Preparation Time: 20 minutes Cooking Time: 28 minutes

Ingredients:

- Ground Coriander Seed, 1 tsp.
- Cooking Spray, 1 second
- Garam Masala, 1 tsp.
- Fish Fillets, 2 pieces, thawed
- Turmeric, ½ tsp.
- Onions, 2 medium pieces, diced
- Garlic, 3 cloves, minced
- Green Chilies, 2 pieces, seeded and chopped
- Fennel Seeds, ½ tsp.
- Dried Cumin Seed, ½ tsp.
- Balsamic Vinegar, 1 tbsp.
- Canned Tomatoes, 1 can, chopped
- Fish Stock, 2 cups
- Water, 3 cups, hot
- Salt
- Black Pepper, freshly ground

- Cilantro Leaves, 4 sprigs

Procedure:

1. Poach the fish fillets in the soup maker with the 3 cups hot water. While the fish poaches, spray a skillet with the cooking spray and sauté the onions, garlic and chilies until softened and aromatic. Toast the spices for 3 minutes and add these along with the other ingredients except the cilantro leaves into the soup maker. Secure the lid.
2. Program for Chunky, timed at 21 minutes. Once the soup is cooked, transfer into bowls and garnish with the cilantro. Serve immediately.

Nutritional Facts: Cal: 481; Carb: 43.2g; Protein: 64g; Fat: 7.9g; Fiber: 9.9g; Sugars: 12.5g; Cholesterol: 127mg; Sodium: 1252mg

7.24 Oriental Tuna Soup

Serves: 2 Preparation Time: 5 minutes Cooking Time: 21 minutes

Ingredients:

- Tofu, 1 block, diced
- Tuna, canned in brine, drained
- Scallions, 1 bunch, trimmed and sliced
- Miso, 2 **tbsp.**s
- Chicken Stock Cubes, 2 pieces
- Water, 5 cups
- Soy Sauce, 1 **tbsp.**

Procedure:

1. Add all of the ingredients except the soy sauce into the soup maker and secure the lid. Program the soup maker for Chunky timed at 21 minutes. Once the soup has finished cooking, carefully lift the lid and stir in the soy sauce. Transfer into bowls and serve immediately.

Nutritional Facts: Cal: 530; Carb: 18.1g; Protein: 63.8g; Fat: 22.5g; Fiber: 3.5g; Sugars: 3.5g; Cholesterol: 56mg; Sodium: 4628mg

7.25 Portuguese Fish Soup

Serves: 4 Preparation Time: 5 minutes Cooking Time: 25 minutes

Ingredients:

- Carrot, 1 large piece, peeled and diced
- Potatoes, 2 medium pieces, peeled and cubed
- Red Bell Pepper, 1 small piece, seeded and chopped
- White Fish, 100 grams fillet
- Clam Meat, 100 grams
- Prawns, 100 grams, shelled and deveined
- Canned Tomatoes, 1 can, chopped
- Red Wine, 1/3 cup
- Garlic Paste, 2 **tsp.**
- Mustard, 1 **tsp.**
- Paprika, 2 **tsp.**
- Water, ¼ cup
- Salt
- Black Pepper, freshly ground

Procedure:

1. Add the diced carrots, peppers and potatoes into the soup maker. Dice the white fish fillets and add into the soup maker along with the remainder of the ingredients. Stir to combine and secure the lid. Set for Chunky timed at 25 minutes. Garnish with thyme.

Nutritional Facts: Cal: 190; Carb: 19g; Protein: 14g; Fat: 0g; Fiber: 4g; Sugars: 2g; Cholesterol: 76mg; Sodium: 271mg

7.26 Back to Basics Fish Stew

Serves: 4 Preparation Time: 10 minutes Cooking Time: 20 minutes

Ingredients:

- Clam Juice, 2 cups
- Cod Fillets, 8 oz., cut into ½ inch cubes
- Canned Tomatoes, chopped
- Onion, ½ cup, chopped
- Celery, ½ cup, chopped
- Thyme Leaves, dried, ½ **tsp.**
- Garlic, 1 clove, minced
- Salt
- Black Pepper, freshly ground
- Parsley Leaves, fresh, 2 **tbsp.**s, chopped

Procedure:

1. Add all of the ingredients into the soup maker and secure the lid. Program for chunky timed at 21 minutes. Once the stew has been fully cooked, transfer into bowls and garnish with parsley. Serve immediately.

Nutritional Facts: Cal: 370; Carb: 40.8g; Protein: 44.4g; Fat: 2.8g; Fiber: 3.8g; Sugars: 12g; Cholesterol: 110mg; Sodium: 1055mg

7.27 Cullen Skink

Serves: 1 Preparation Time: 10 minutes Cooking Time: 21 minutes

Ingredients:

- Potatoes, 1 ½ cups, peeled and diced
- Haddock, 4 oz.
- Water, 2 cups
- Onions, ¼ cup, chopped
- Skim Milk, 2 cups
- Salt
- Black Pepper, freshly ground

Procedure:

1. Poach the haddock in water for 4 minutes until the fish is fully cooked. Remove the haddock from the poaching liquid and reserve the liquid. Add the potatoes, onions, haddock and a cup of the fish stock into the soup maker. Add the skimmed milk, and season with salt and pepper. Secure the lid and program for smooth, timed at 21 minutes. Once cooked, transfer into bowls and serve immediately.

Nutritional Facts: Cal: 405; Carb: 45.5g; Protein: 46.9g; Fat: 1.2g; Fiber: 3.6g; Sugars: 27g; Cholesterol: 97mg; Sodium: 1301mg

7.28 Crustacean Corn Soup

Serves: 4 Preparation Time: 5 minutes Cooking Time: 21 minutes

Ingredients:

- Canned Corn Kernels, 1 can, drained and rinsed
- Creamed Corn, 1 can,
- Pumpkin, 1 wedge, cubed
- Onion, 1 small, peeled and chopped
- Garlic, 1 clove, crushed
- White Wine, 1 cup
- Vegetable Stock, 2 cups
- Salt
- Garlic Butter, ¼ cup
- Prawns, 12 pieces, shelled and deveined

Procedure:

1. Add the corn, pumpkin, onion, garlic, wine and stock into the soup maker. Season with salt and stir to combine. Secure the lid and program for smooth for 21 minutes. While the soup cooks, heat the butter in a skillet and cook the prawns until curled up and lightly browned.
2. Once the soup is cooked, use the blender function of the soup maker until it reaches the desired consistency. Transfer into bowls and top with the cooked prawns. Serve immediately.

Nutritional Facts: Cal: 1418; Carb: 149.3g; Protein: 111g; Fat: 43.1g; Fiber: 11.9g; Sugars: 31.5g; Cholesterol: 945mg; Sodium: 4954mg

7.29 Prawn Tom Yam

Serves: 4 Preparation Time: 10 minutes Cooking Time: 8 minutes

Ingredients:

- Chicken Stock, 3 cups
- Tom Yam Paste, 1 **tbsp.**
- Scallions, 3 stalks, peeled and chopped
- Lemon Grass, 1 stalk, inner leaves finely chopped
- Lime Juice from 1 lime
- Fish Sauce, 2 **tbsp.**s
- Palm Sugar, 1 **tsp.**
- Button Mushrooms, ¼ cup, thinly sliced
- Prawns, 7 oz., shelled and deveined
- Cilantro, finely chopped

Procedure:

1. Add all of the ingredients except the prawns and cilantro into the soup maker and secure the lid. Use the simmer function for 5 minutes and let the soup maker stir. Add the prawns and allow to cook for another 3 minutes on simmer until cooked. Transfer into bowls and garnish with cilantro. Serve immediately.

Nutritional Facts: Cal: 925; Carb: 48.7g; Protein: 138.7g; Fat: 21.8g; Fiber: 3g; Sugars: 9.3g; Cholesterol: 1155mg; Sodium: 10325mg

7.30 Smoked Haddock Chowder

Serves: 4 Preparation Time: 10 minutes Cooking Time: 30 minutes

Ingredients:

- Butter, 1 **tbsp.**
- Leek, 1 small stalk, rinsed and sliced
- Onion, 1 small piece, peeled and diced
- Whole Milk, 2 cups
- Fish Stock, 1 cup
- Potatoes, 2 medium pieces, peeled and cubed
- Sweet Corn Kernels, ½ cup
- Smoked Haddock Fillets, 500 grams, skinned and cut into pieces
- Double Cream, 4 **tbsp.**s
- Parsley Leaves, 2 **tbsp.**s, chopped

Procedure:

1. Preset the soup maker to 30 minutes on a high setting. Add the butter into the soup maker and allow to melt before the onions and leeks are added. This will take 1-3 minutes. Use the stir function to move the onions and leeks around. Add the milk, fish stock and cubed potatoes and allow the mixture to boil then let the soup simmer for 10-15 minutes.
2. Add the sweet corn kernels and stir. Add the haddock and cook for an additional 10-15 minutes. Blend the soup. Add the double cream and adjust the seasonings. Let the soup cook through and serve in individual bowls. Garnish with parsley.

Nutritional Facts: Cal: 1572; Carb: 125.7g; Protein: 147g; Fat: 56.6g; Fiber: 15.1g; Sugars: 39.6g; Cholesterol: 164mg; Sodium: 963mg

7.31 Thai Coconut and Prawn Broth

Serves: 4 Preparation Time: 10 minutes Cooking Time: 15 minutes

Ingredients:

- Peanut Oil, 1 **tbsp.**
- Onion, 1 small piece, finely chopped
- Ginger, fresh, 3 **tsp.**, grated
- Garlic, 2 cloves, peeled and crushed
- Thai Green Curry Paste, 2 **tbsp.**s
- Coconut Milk, 1 can
- Fish Sauce, 1 **tbsp.**
- Palm Sugar, 1 **tsp.**
- Prawns, 150 grams
- Basil Leaves, ½ cup, shredded

Procedure:

1. Set the Soup Maker on simmer for 4 minutes. Allow the peanut oil to heat up and cook the onion, ginger and garlic for 1-3 minutes. Use the stir function to cook these. Add the curry paste and cook for a minute. Pour the coconut milk, fish sauce and palm sugar into the soup maker and puree the soup until smooth. Allow to cook on low for 4-5 minutes.
2. Set the soup maker on simmer for 9 minutes. Add the prawns after five minutes and cook until the timer elapses. Stir in the basil leaves and transfer into bowls. Serve immediately.

Nutritional Facts: Cal: 1206; Carb: 39.1g; Protein: 47.4g; Fat: 101.5g; Fiber: 10.3g; Sugars: 20g; Cholesterol: 332mg; Sodium: 2073mg

7.32 Cauliflower Crab Cream Chowder

Serves: 1 Preparation Time: 10 minutes Cooking Time: 30 minutes

Ingredients:

- Cauliflower, 1 medium head
- Crab Meat, from 1 crab
- White Wine, 1 glass
- Bacon, 8 slices
- Cheddar Cheese, 50 grams, shredded
- Mustard, 2 **tsp.**
- Garlic Paste, 2 **tsp.**
- Parsley Leaves, fresh, 2 **tsp.**
- Fish Stock, 1 cup
- Chives, 2 **tsp.**, chopped
- Lemon Juice, 1 **tbsp.**
- Salt
- Black Pepper, freshly ground

Procedure:

1. Add the all of the ingredients except for the lemon juice and chives into the soup maker. Secure the lid and program for smooth, set for 28 minutes. Once the soup is fully cooked, lift the lid and stir in the lemon juice. Transfer into bowls and garnish with chives. Serve immediately.

Nutritional Facts: Cal: 1462; Carb: 41.3g; Protein: 99.6g; Fat: 90.4g; Fiber: 15.6g; Sugars: 16.2g; Cholesterol: 274mg; Sodium: 5142mg

7.33 Simple Prawn Broth

Serves: 4 Preparation Time: 5 minutes Cooking Time: 28 minutes

Ingredients:

- Prawns, 4 oz., shelled and deveined
- Onion, 1 medium piece, chopped
- Tomato Puree, 1 **tbsp.**
- Fish Stock, 4 cups
- Tomatoes, 2 pieces, chopped
- Garlic, 1 clove, crushed
- Mixed Herbs, 1 **tsp.**
- Crème Fraiche, 3 **tbsp.**s

Procedure:

1. Add all of the ingredients except for the crème fraiche into the soup maker, but reserve some of the prawns for garnish. Program the soup maker for smooth and set for 28 minutes. Once the soup has been fully cooked, transfer into bowls and top with the crème fraiche. Poach the remaining prawns in lightly seasoned water until just opaque and set on top of the crème fraiche. Serve immediately.

Nutritional Facts: Cal: 156; Carb: 4.37g; Protein: 18.3g; Fat: 7.1g; Fiber: 1g; Sugars: 2.8g; Cholesterol: 285mg; Sodium: 471mg

7.34 Southern Seafood Bisque

Serves: 4 Preparation Time: 5 minutes Cooking Time: 30 minutes

Ingredients:

- Unsalted Butter, 3 **tbsp.**s
- Onion, 2 **tbsp.**s, chopped
- Celery, 2 **tbsp.**s, chopped
- Flour, 3 **tbsp.**s
- Whole Milk, 2 ½ cups
- Black Pepper
- Tomato Paste, 1 **tbsp.**
- Heavy Cream, 1 cup
- Cooked Shrimp, 8 oz.,
- Crab Meat, 8 oz.,
- Sherry, 2 **tbsp.**s
- Parsley Leaves, fresh, 3 **tbsp.**s, chopped

Procedure:

1. Heat the butter in a saucepan over a medium flame and sauté the onions and celery until softened, about 2 minutes. Add the flour into this mixture and stir to form a roux. Cook for about 2 minutes. Heat the milk in a saucepan over a medium flame, and gradually mix the milk into the roux until the milk has thickened. Add this into the soup maker and add the pepper, tomato paste and cream. Secure the lid, program for smooth and set the time for 28 minutes.
2. Once the soup has cooked, stir in the shrimp, crab meat and sherry. Use the blender function to puree the soup to your desired consistency. Transfer into bowls and garnish with the parsley. Serve immediately.

Nutritional Facts: Cal: 501; Carb: 16g; Protein: 31g; Fat: 35g; Fiber: 1g; Sugars: 10g; Cholesterol: 277mg; Sodium: 902mg

7.35 Prawn Bisque (35)

Serves: 4 Preparation Time: 5 minutes Cooking Time: 23 minutes

Ingredients:

- Prawns, 200 grams, shelled and deveined
- Tomato, 1 piece, chopped
- Leek, 1 piece, rinsed and chopped
- Garlic, 1 clove, peeled and chopped
- Onion, 1 small piece, peeled and chopped
- Tomato Paste, 1 **tbsp.**
- Cayenne Pepper, 1 **tsp.**
- Fish Stock, 2 cups
- Heavy Cream, ½ cup
- Saffron
- Salt

Procedure:

1. Chop the tomato and leeks and add them into the soup maker with the remainder of the ingredients except the saffron. Make sure that the prawns are the topmost layer. Secure the lid and program for smooth at 28 minutes. Once the soup has been cooked, transfer into bowls and serve immediately.

Nutritional Facts: Cal: 1079; Carb: 35g; Protein: 112.7g; Fat: 53.8g; Fiber: 6.5g; Sugars: 13.5g; Cholesterol: 1052mg; Sodium: 1990mg

8 10-WEEK MEAL PLAN

Week 1

	Breakfast	Lunch	Supper
Day 1	Chickpea Soup	Beef and Pasta Soup	Scotch Broth
Day 2	Gazpacho	Leftover Chickpea Soup	French Onion Soup
Day 3	Leftover Scotch Broth	Mulligatawny	Leftover Gazpacho
Day 4	Cream of Asparagus Soup	Porky Bean Soup	Cullen Skink
Day 5	Leftover Porky Bean Soup	Leftover Cullen Skink	Fish Curry
Day 6	Leftover Cream of Asparagus Soup	Simple Prawn Broth	Seafood Noodle Soup
Day 7	Cream of Mushroom Soup	Leftover Seafood Noodle Soup	Leftover Prawn Broth

Week 2

	Breakfast	Lunch	Supper
Day 1	Quick Vichysoisse	Chicken and Mushroom Soup	Quick Lobster Bisque
Day 2	Pea Potage	Leftover Chicken and Mushroom Soup	Leftover Bisque
Day 3	Spring Vegetable Soup	Quickfire Crab Bisque	Avocado Bacon Soup
Day 4	Leftover Vichysoisse	Leftover Avocado Bacon Soup	London Fog Soup
Day 5	Leftover Spring Vegetable Soup	Leftover Crab Bisque	Ham and Corn Chowder
Day 6	Left Over Pea Potage	Leftover London Fog Soup	Winter Chicken Soup
Day 7	Summer Corn Chowder	Leftover Winter Chicken Soup	Leftover Corn Chowder

Week 3

	Breakfast	Lunch	Supper
Day 1	Apple and Parsnip Potage	Mexican Taco Soup	Beef Vegetable Soup
Day 2	Bulgur and Bean Soup	Leftover Beef Vegetable Soup	Leftover Taco Soup
Day 3	Sweetened Parsnip Soup	Chili Chicken Soup	Tilapia Soup
Day 4	Vegetable Soup	Leftover Tilapia Soup	Leftover Chili Chicken Soup
Day 5	Potato Pepper Pot	Leftover Vegetable Soup	Smoked Haddock Chowder
Day 6	Leftover Apple and Parsnip Potage	Leftover Haddock Chowder	Shrimp and Mushroom Bisque
Day 7	Leftover Parsnip Soup	Bacon and Lentil Soup	Halibut Soup

Week 4

	Breakfast	Lunch	Supper
Day 1	Scotch Broth	Minestrone with Meatballs	Southwestern Chicken Soup
Day 2	Carrot Curry Soup	Leftover Southwestern Chicken Soup	Leftover Minestrone
Day 3	Scotch Broth	Irish Bacon Soup	New England Style Cod Soup
Day 4	Carrot Curry Soup	Leftover Cod Soup	Leftover Irish Bacon Soup
Day 5	Scotch Broth	Chorizo and Bean Soup	Summer Squash Shrimp Soup
Day 6	Spring Vegetable Soup	Leftover Summer Squash Soup	Leftover Chorizo and Bean Soup
Day 7	Scotch Broth	Lox and Schmear Soup	Leftover Lox and Schmear Soup

Week 5

	Breakfast	Lunch	Supper
Day 1	Snow Pea and Shrimp Broth	Summer Salmon Broth	Potato Pork Potage
Day 2	Leftover Salmon Broth	Leftover Snow Pea Broth	Pork and Barley Soup
Day 3	Leftover Potato Pork Potage	Prawn Tom Yam	Leftover Pork and Barley Soup
Day 4	Cullen Skink	Leftover Prawn Tom Yam	Mock Chili Relleno Soup
Day 5	Levantine Chicken Soup	Leftover Cullen Skink	Leftover Chili Relleno Soup
Day 6	Beef Burgundy Soup	Spring Lamb Soup	Beans con Carne Soup
Day 7	Leftover Spring Lamb Soup	Leftover Beef Burgundy Soup	Leftover Spring Lamb Soup

Week 6

	Breakfast	Lunch	Supper
Day 1	Prawn Bisque	Seafood Noodle Soup	Mediterranean Lamb Soup
Day 2	Chicken Corn Chowder	Warming Pepper Soup	Bacon and Pasta Soup
Day 3	Leftover Chicken Corn Chowder	Leftover Lamb Soup	Leftover Prawn Bisque
Day 4	Leftover Seafood Noodle Soup	Leftover Warming Pepper Soup	Leftover Bacon and Pasta Soup
Day 5	Bourbonnaise Cream Soup	Spanish Chicken Soup	Potato Pepper Pot
Day 6	Cheesy Cauliflower Soup	Mixed Vegetable Borscht	Eastern Salmon Soup
Day 7	Leftover Potato Pepper Pot	Leftover Bourbonnaise Cream Soup	Leftover Vegetable Borscht

Week 7

	Breakfast	Lunch	Supper
Day 1	Sausage and Gnocchi Soup	Creamy Salmon Chowder	Bacon and Lentil Soup
Day 2	Bacalhau con Tomate Soup	Crustacean Corn Soup	Gazpacho
Day 3	Leftover Gazpacho	Leftover Salmon Chowder	Leftover Gnocchi Soup
Day 4	Leftover Bacon and Lentil Soup	Leftover Crustacean Corn Soup	Leftover Bacalhau con Tomate Soup
Day 5	Pea Potage	Beefy Pulse Soup	Herbed Poultry Potage
Day 6	Spiced Irish Lamb Soup	Leftover Pea Potage	Leftover Beefy Pulse Soup
Day 7	Cream of Chicken Soup	Green Pasture Soup	British Broccoli Soup

Week 8

	Breakfast	Lunch	Supper
Day 1	Carrot and Cilantro Soup	Beefy Noodle Soup	Mock Bolognese Soup
Day 2	Indian Pasta Soup	Wild Rice and Turkey Soup	Asian Chicken Noodle Soup
Day 3	Tomato and Coconut Soup	Leftover Beefy Noodle Soup	Leftover Mock Bolognese Soup
Day 4	Leftover Chicken Noodle Soup	Leftover Indian Pasta Soup	Leftover Wild Rice and Turkey Soup
Day 5	Cream of Broccoli Soup	Leftover Carrot and Cilantro Soup	Green Pork and Beans Soup
Day 6	Ham and Bean Pottage	Roast Chicken Soup	Leftover Cream of Broccoli Soup
Day 7	Spiced Pumpkin Potage	London Fog Soup	Leftover Ham and Bean Pottage

Week 9

	Breakfast	Lunch	Supper
Day 1	Hearty Potato Bacon Chowder	Portuguese Fish Soup	Cauliflower Chicken Cream Soup
Day 2	Chili Chicken Soup	Oriental Beef Soup	Summer Corn Chowder
Day 3	Leftover Potato Bacon Chowder	Leftover Cauliflower Cream Soup	Leftover Summer Corn Chowder
Day 4	Leftover Portuguese Fish Soup	Leftover Chili Chicken Soup	Leftover Oriental Beef Soup
Day 5	London Fog Soup	Bacon Vichysoisse	Southern Split Pea Ham Soup
Day 6	Chicken and Corn Soup	Spring Lamb Soup	French Onion Soup
Day 7	Leftover French Onion Soup	Leftover London Fog Soup	Leftover Bacon Vichysoisse

Week 10

	Breakfast	Lunch	Supper
Day 1	Cream of Mushroom Soup	Winter Root Vegetable Soup	Ham and Corn Chowder
Day 2	Irish Bacon Soup	Scotch Broth	Bacon and Lentil Soup
Day 3	Leftover Ham and Corn Chowder	Leftover Bacon and Lentil Soup	Leftover Cream of Mushroom Soup
Day 4	Leftover Irish Bacon Soup	Leftover Winter Root Vegetable Soup	Leftover Scotch Broth
Day 5	Mixed Vegetable Borscht	Beef Burgundy Soup	Creamy Mushroom Soup
Day 6	Pumpkin Curry Soup with Dukkha	Porky Bean Soup	Mock Chili Relleno Soup
Day 7	Leftover Creamy Mushroom Soup	Leftover Porky Bean Soup	Leftover Mock Chili Relleno Soup

8.1 APPENDICES

8.2 To Convert to Metric

Unit	Multiply By	Result
Tsp.	4.93	Milliliters
Tablespoons	14.79	
Fluid Ounces	29.57	
Cups	236.59	
Cups	0.236	Liters
Quarts	0.946	
Gallons	3.785	
Ounces	28.35	Grams
Pounds	0.454	Kilograms
Inches	2.54	Centimeters
Fahrenheit	Subtract 32, times 5, divided by 9	Celsius

8.3 To Convert from Metric

Unit	Divide By	To Get
Milliliters	4.93	**Tsp.**
	14.79	**Tbsp.**s
	29.57	Fluid Ounces
	236.59	Cups
	473.18	Pints
	946.36	Quarts
Liters	0.236	Cups
	0.473	Pints
	0.946	Quarts
	3.785	Gallons
Grams	28.35	Ounces
Kilograms	.454	Pounds
Centimeters	2.54	Inches
Celsius	Multiply by 9, Divide by 5, add 32	Fahrenheit

Printed in Great Britain
by Amazon

17128760R00054